SHAPING EDUCATIONAL POLICY

Books by James Bryant Conant

SHAPING EDUCATIONAL POLICY
THE AMERICAN HIGH SCHOOL TODAY
THE CHILD, THE PARENT, AND THE STATE
EDUCATION IN THE JUNIOR HIGH SCHOOL
  YEARS
SLUMS AND SUBURBS
THE EDUCATION OF AMERICAN TEACHERS

SHAPING
EDUCATIONAL
POLICY

JAMES BRYANT CONANT

McGRAW-HILL BOOK COMPANY
New York   Toronto   London

SHAPING EDUCATIONAL POLICY

THE CARNEGIE SERIES IN AMERICAN EDUCATION

The books in this series have resulted from studies made under grants from the Carnegie Corporation of New York and from time to time studies supported by The Carnegie Foundation for the Advancement of Teaching. These books are published by McGraw-Hill in recognition of their importance to the future of American education.

The Corporation, a philanthropic foundation established in 1911 by Andrew Carnegie for the advancement and diffusion of knowledge and understanding, has a continuing interest in the improvement of American education. It financed the studies in this series to provide facts and recommendations which would be useful to all those who make or influence the decisions which shape American educational policies and institutions.

The statements made and views expressed in these books are solely the responsibility of the authors.

Books Published

Berelson · Graduate Education in the United States
Clark · The Open Door College: A Case Study
Cleveland · The Overseas American
Conant · The American High School Today
Conant · The Education of American Teachers
Conant · Shaping Educational Policy
Corson · Governance of Colleges and Universities
Dodds · The Academic President—Educator or Caretaker?
Glenny · Autonomy of Public Colleges
Henninger · The Technical Institute in America
Kitzhaber · Themes, Theories, and Therapy: The Teaching of
    Writing in College
McConnell · A General Pattern for American Public Higher Education
    cation
Medsker · The Junior College: Progress and Prospect
Perkins and Snell · The Education of Historians in the United
    States
Pierson · The Education of American Businessmen
Thomas · The Search for a Common Learning: General Education,
    tion, 1800–1960
Weidner · The World Role of Universities

ACKNOWLEDGMENT

The writing of this volume would have been impossible without the extended assistance of Professor Nicholas A. Masters of Pennsylvania State University. As a political scientist who had studied both state and national governmental structures, he was able to guide my study of the relation of education to politics in the sixteen most populous states of the Union during the last year of my two-year study of the education of American teachers. The pages which follow are in a sense a by-product of that study. In acknowledging my indebtedness to Professor Masters for his help in preparing the manuscript, as well as his skillful appraisal of many complicated situations, I wish to make it plain that he is not responsible for the opinions or recommendations contained in this book. The responsibility for what follows is entirely my own.

James Bryant Conant

May, 1964
New York, N.Y.

CONTENTS

CHAPTER 1

Education Becomes
a National Concern

All over the world today national governments are considering educational problems in revolutionary terms. These terms differ somewhat from country to country, but the revolutionary basis is much the same in all free, highly industrialized large countries. An influential body of public opinion has become convinced that the nation is suffering from a shortage of highly educated persons. There is a widespread feeling that much potential talent has been lost because it has not been developed by the schools and the institutions of higher education. Directing attention particularly to engineers and scientists, one can easily demonstrate that such a situation endangers a nation's industrial capacity and may endanger even its military security.

1

The Concurrent Educational Revolutions

The fact that this concern is so widespread makes it easy to speak of a worldwide educational revolution. But the phrase "educational revolution" means different things in different countries. There are, in fact, several revolutions. In Great Britain, in France, and in free Germany the proposed revolution includes the expansion of the schools for those 16 and 17 years of age who are not intending to enter a university. The demand for an educational system that, in terms of enrollments at least, is more like our system in the United States is an interesting phenomenon, particularly to an American observer. The arguments in favor of this step are similar to those one heard in this country fifty years ago. One might call them social or political arguments. They are closely related to a desire to use public education as an instrument for diminishing the degree of social stratification of society. This point of view comes out clearly in some of the current discussions in the nations I have named. To these arguments a new set have been added by certain American and European economists who have shown a relationship between the material prosperity of a nation (or of an American group of states) and the degree of education of the population.

For those who remember the high rate of unemployment in the learned professions in the 1930s, it is strange that so little heed is given to the possibility of a recurrence of unemployment among certain groups of highly educated persons. But the demand for more and better education at all levels is based on *both* a belief in democratic principles and a concern with a national shortage of well-trained people. The two arguments together are today so powerful as to sweep aside any doubts that might be expressed as to whether in the 1980s we might have too many scientists in one specialized branch or another. In a free society it is easier to bury such thoughts than to face up to the possibilities of attempting to forecast national needs and persuading able young people to go into one profession rather than another.

In Great Britain, France, and free Germany the universities have been the focus of the most intense criticism. Plans are now well developed in these three nations for a large expansion in the number of university students. In the United States it has been the schools and colleges (not the universities in the European sense of the word, i.e., the graduate and professional schools) that have been most heavily criticized. Many people have expressed the opinion that what we need in this country is both an increase in the fraction of our youth who attend college and an improvement in the education offered. There can be no doubt that many of our public schools have failed to challenge the intellectual ambitions of many able pupils; many of our high schools have not offered the opportunities for study which are essential for the development of scientific and scholarly talent. The situation has improved over the last ten years, but there are still demands for profound and far-reaching changes in both our public schools and our colleges.

On the public school level, many who would agree that something like an educational revolution was in progress in the United States would have in mind revolutionary changes in methods of instruction. Such words as television, team teaching, language laboratories, teaching machines, and programmed instruction would come to mind. Such thoughts are not unrelated to the demand for the improvement of education. One hopes that in the future a larger percentage of the intellectually able will be ready for advanced studies in the graduate departments of our universities. Some laymen might be inclined to speak of making our schools and colleges more "efficient." By which may be meant either that one able teacher can teach a far greater number of pupils than at present or that a pupil may

acquire a certain block of knowledge or develop a given
skill more rapidly than in the past. We shall meet both
points of view in later chapters. There can be no doubt that
the introduction of new methods of teaching has already
introduced complications into the American public school
picture. *It is my belief there will be more radical changes in
the future and this in turn means that our old methods of
determining educational policy need drastic revision to
meet the impact of the educational revolutions.*

Let me give at this point only two or three illustrations
to support my conclusion. In subsequent chapters I shall
amplify and expand my thesis that the national concern for
education and the revolution in techniques have together
made obsolete our past methods of determining educational
policy in the United States. Take the high school
curriculum, for example. With the exception of certain
schools in certain localities, those who determined policy in
the 1930s and 1940s were primarily concerned with education for democracy, and placed great emphasis first on the
development of those attitudes that were believed essential
to citizens of a free society and second on the free development of a wide range of skills among all pupils. The contrast
between what was recommended and the old-fashioned
"purely academic" curriculum was underlined in books and
articles by professors of education and forward-looking
educational administrators. One could hardly quarrel with
this emphasis in a period of our history when free societies
were threatened all over the world. But one consequence
was that the content of the academic high school curriculum made little difference. This was convenient in a
society as geographically mobile as our own. A family could
move from one city to another or from one state to another
and the children could be placed in a new school with little
inconvenience. The educators who were determining public
high school policy in those days seemed to have in mind that
a real differentiation in the areas of study should be

postponed until *after* high school. Time enough when one enters college to concentrate on mathematics beyond algebra or a foreign language or chemistry or physics or a study in depth of American history. I often heard such arguments in the 1940s and even in the 1950s.

Our highly decentralized control of secondary education, with more than 4,000 school boards determining the offerings, is quite incomprehensible to most Europeans (even those who admire our comprehensive high schools). I recall a group of German schoolteachers and administrators expressing amazement that pupils could transfer so readily from one school to another in the United States. An experienced leader of American public school teachers who was taking part in the conversation replied in a half-joking manner, "Oh, there are no difficulties with us in the United States, because from your point of view as Germans we don't teach the pupils anything, even in our high schools."

Behind the joke lies a hard core of reality. The people whose efforts made possible the development of the comprehensive high school in this century were not much interested in either foreign languages or in the *early* development of mathematical skills and knowledge. They were interested in the three R's (though their critics have denied this) and in the development of attitudes favorable to the continuation and improvement of our free society. Thus a common denominator of studies suitable for all types of ability and a variety of ambitions was relatively easily identified. A curriculum in each school which could be identical for all pupils was also a curriculum which could be identical in all schools. Such a curriculum became standard. There was little difficulty in children moving from one school to another until the senior high school was reached.

At the senior high school level the elective principle introduced the required flexibility. Provided the optional courses were the same from one school to another, transfer from one district to another was a matter of little difficulty. To be sure unless a high school is of sufficient size (approximately 300–500 pupils), it is extremely unlikely that a variety of optional courses will be offered. Therefore transfer from large high schools to small high schools has never been as easy as the corresponding shift in the lower grades. Still, by and large until the end of World War II, one might say that the degree of uniformity in school curricula and procedures in grades 1–12 was sufficient so that parental complaints about difficulty of moving from one school to another were the least of the worries of school administrators.

The educational revolution has rapidly changed the situation. Foreign languages are now being taught in the lower grades. This fact introduces complications. One school district may offer French (and only French) in grades 3–8, another may offer only Spanish. When parents move from one district to another, such facts produce unpleasant complications. We have been proud of our highly decentralized public school system. We have boasted about the flexibility of the system, which allowed for so much independence and experimentation. To date the children have not paid too high a price for this diversity. But I foresee that the time when the revolutionary changes in the school curricula, with increasing emphasis on the sequential subjects—foreign languages and mathematics— will produce so much diversity that the public will demand that some order be restored by one method or another.

The old mechanisms that influenced the growth of the curricula in the public schools are no longer operating as they once did. This fact alone is a challenge to the American public and American educators to consider how to plan for the future. An even greater challenge is that presented by the growth of the advanced placement movement. In a word, this is a scheme by which academically talented students are able to complete freshman college work in the last year in high school. Whether such courses are in the area hitherto considered the preserve of the public school people or whether they are subject to control by subject matter professors (of English or chemistry, for example) can be debated. What is clear is that the old line that separated the high school from college is now a fuzzy transition zone.

I think it is easy to demonstrate that educational policy for our public schools has been largely determined by educators concerned directly with the schools or those who were involved in introducing the teachers to the art and science of teaching. Implementation was often a matter for the chief state school officer and the superintendents of the larger districts. Year books, articles in educational journals, and such publications as those of the Educational Policies Commission reflected the thinking of the leaders of what I and others have called the "educational establishment." I am not one of the harsh critics of the establishment. Indeed I was a member of the Policies Commission off and on for twenty-two years. In retrospect I think it clear that the educational establishment was not as responsive as it should have been to the changing attitudes of the public toward education. A comparison of the document published by the Policies Commission in 1950 entitled "Education for the Gifted" with the program recommended by a conference on the education of the "Academically Talented" (called by the N E A) in 1958 is instructive. For the *highly* gifted (1 per cent of the population) the commission recommended in 1950 an academic program which the conference in 1958 thought proper for the upper quarter of the high school student body! To be sure, in 1950 the commission had said:

Many *moderately* gifted students could also profit from more social studies, advanced mathematics, and foreign languages in high school; but in their case the need is neither so clear nor so compelling as it is in the case of the highly gifted.

As late as 1958, however, the commission was writing about the education of the gifted as follows:[1]

> Gifted pupils should be identified early and given early opportunities to challenge their powers and develop their talents to the fullest. . . . In high schools, courses of study should be designed to allow the able students to carry heavier loads in balanced programs which include mathematics, science, and languages, together with English, social studies, and humanities. . . . Advanced courses, however, should not be imposed on students who lack the required talent.

Unfortunately in this document we did not redefine the word "gifted" and therefore left the implication that we were writing about only 1 per cent of the population at a time when the NEA conference came out for a broad, rigorous academic program for the academically talented— some 20 or 25 per cent of the population.

But leaving aside all criticisms of the past, it seems clear that any amorphous unofficial body composed of public school administrators and professors of education is not now well suited to establishing policy for our public schools. I know from my experiences in many committee meetings that it was easy to outline principles for secondary education as long as one focussed attention on "democratic living" and the relation of school to the "world of work." But when it comes to deciding whether or not instruction in a foreign language should be made compulsory in grade 3 and higher and which language, then the organizations of public school people are not in a position to provide helpful guidelines. I conclude therefore that we must consider a drastic alteration in the ways in which educational policy for our public schools is shaped. The next chapter is devoted to a further consideration of this topic.

[1] *The Contemporary Challenge to American Education*, p. 10.

Education Beyond the High School

On the level of college and graduate schools, the American educational revolution is quite different from the revolution taking place in the public schools. Where post-high-school education is concerned, at the moment, public attention is directed to the problem of expanding our post-high-school facilities to accommodate the large increase in potential college students resulting from the baby boom in the 1940s. The national government, recognizing the serious nature of the problem, enacted legislation in December 1963 authorizing loans and grants to aid in the construction of buildings for higher education.[1]

The Organization for Economic Cooperation and Development has undertaken a review of national policies for science and education to assist member countries[2] reassessing their programs. A review of the United States which was published in November 1963 is primarily concerned with problems of higher education in relation to

[1] Section 2 of the Act reads as follows:
The Congress hereby finds that the security and welfare of the United States require that this and future generations of American youth be assured ample opportunity for the fullest development of their intellectual capacities, and that this opportunity will be jeopardized unless the Nation's colleges and universities are encouraged and assisted in their efforts to accommodate rapidly growing numbers of youth who aspire to a higher education. The Congress further finds and declares that these needs are so great and these steps so urgent that it is incumbent upon the Nation to take positive and immediate action to meet these needs through assistance to institutions of higher education, including graduate and undergraduate institutions, junior and community colleges, and technical institutes, in providing certain academic facilities.

[2] The member countries of O E C D are: Austria, Belgium, Canada, Denmark, France, the Federal Republic of Germany, Greece, Iceland, Ireland, Italy, Luxemburg, the Netherlands, Norway, Portugal, Spain, Sweden, Switzerland, Turkey, the United Kingdom, and the United States.

future demands for scientific and technological manpower. It is a most interesting document and deserves careful attention by all citizens concerned with the welfare of the United States. I shall refer to it more than once in the pages that follow. In a few pages the authors present a concise picture of American higher education. (Two of their tabular compilations are so illuminating that I am reproducing them as Tables 1 and 2 on pages 12 and 13.) They then write as follows:

> The foregoing sketchy outline of American higher education leaves us doubting whether it can be properly called a system. There is, for example, no powerful centralising and unifying force comparable with that in France or Russia or the United Kingdom. Instead, there is competition between many different state and private ventures and which, in the past at least, has served America well. Of course, as we shall see, the extent of federal involvement is immense and growing rapidly. *The question in our minds is whether the solution of the approaching manpower crisis and the further advance of the United States into what we have called the third stage of education development will not require more explicit organising action by state and federal agencies* [italics mine].

A few paragraphs later the opinion is expressed that "the need for expansion which now confronts American higher education will put a severe strain on the nation's resources. . . . The next generation of Americans will experience the first fully developed system of universal higher education. Public funds and publicly led coordination, on at least a state-wide basis, will be added to the past autonomy of separate institutions. The scale of organizations will increase. . . ." And in a later section of the same document, three questions are raised: "How can the educational facilities of the country be expanded to meet the demand? How can the teachers be found? How will the bill be paid and by whom?"

Neither the examiners[1] who wrote the report nor the American delegation that later discussed it could provide exact answers to these questions. The 100-page pamphlet, however, contains impressive evidence of the educational revolution which is underway in the United States and which in the national interest must not be halted but, through informed public discussion, must be guided into the most effective channels possible.

One might say, of course, the revolution started in the United States at the close of World War II. Each year since then, increasing amounts of federal funds have been spent to support research in both private and public universities. Table 3 (taken from the O E C D report) sums up the rapid changes which have occurred since 1948. The Federal funds for research and education have increased from $95.3 million to $534.4 million.[2] The fact that 61.5 per cent of all the Federal funds went to only 20 institutions is an illustration of the kind of problem that must be faced because of the revolutionary expansion of Federal research funds for educational institutions. I shall refer to this and related problems in later chapters.

In engineering, in medicine as well as in the physical and biological sciences, it is difficult to separate research from education. Therefore federal support of research on a colossal scale has also amounted in large measure to federal support of education in scientific fields, particularly at the graduate level. Thus the revolution to which I have

[1] The examiners were: Sir John Cockcroft (U.K.), Dr. A. H. Halsey (U.K.), Prof. Ingvar Svennilson (Sweden). The members of the United States delegation included: the Under Secretary of Health, Education and Welfare, an assistant director of the National Science Foundation, an industrialist and two college presidents.

[2] The Federal agencies which have supplied these funds include the Defense Department, the National Institute of Health, and the National Science Foundation, whose establishment in 1951 marked a turning point in American scientific history and also in education.

Table 1. Number of Institutions by Type and Highest Level of Qualification Offered, United States 1961–1962

Type of Programme	Highest Level of Offering					
	Total	A	B	C	D	E
a) **Terminal—Occupational**	56	55	—	—	—	1
b) **Liberal Arts & general**	133	47	67	15	2	2
c) **Liberal Arts & general & terminal occupational**	313	290	21	1	—	1
d) **Primarily teacher preparatory**	116	30	36	47	2	1
e) **Liberal Arts & general & teacher preparatory**	530	41	339	142	6	2
f) **Liberal Arts & general, terminal occup. and teacher preparatory**	261	113	104	40	2	2
g) **Professional or technical**	199	6	72	67	43	11
h) **Professional or technical and teacher preparatory**	77	6	20	32	14	5
i) **Professional or technical and technical occupational**	32	5	18	5	1	3
j) **Liberal Arts & general with 1 or 2 professional schools**	140	—	59	61	16	4
k) **Liberal Arts & general with 3 or more professional schools**	183	—	5	45	133	—
Total	2,040	593	741	455	219	32

A: 2, but less than 4 years, beyond 12th grade
B: Only bachelors and/or first professional degrees
C: Masters' and/or 2nd professional degrees
D: Ph.D. or equivalent
E: Others

Table 2. United States Institutions of Higher Education by Institutional Control and Highest Level of Offering

Type of Control	Highest Level of Offering					
	A	B	C	D	E	Total
PUBLIC:						
State	38	94	162	93	6	393
District or City	308	4	9	6	1	328

PRIVATE:

Independent of Church	115	183	124	71	19	512
Protestant	84	271	92	23	5	475
Roman Catholic	45	181	65	16	1	308
Other	3	8	3	10	—	24
Total	**593**	**741**	**455**	**219**	**32**	**2,040**

A: 2 to 4 years beyond 12th grade
B: Bachelors' and/or first professional degrees
C: Masters' and/or second professional degrees
D: Ph.D. or equivalent
E: Others

Table 3. Concentration of Federal Funds at Educational Institutions, 1948, 1954, and 1958

	Academic Year					
	1947–1948		1953–1954		1957–1958	
	Millions	Per cent	Millions	Per cent	Millions	Per cent
Total Federal Income	528.0	100.0	419.5	100.0	712.4	100.0
Veterans' Tuition and Fees	365.1	69.1	44.4	10.6	5.1	0.7
Land Grant Institutions	43.2	8.2	50.6	12.0	83.9	11.8
Research and Development	95.3	18.0	282.4	67.3	534.4	75.0
Other	24.5	4.6	42.2	10.1	89.0	12.5
Top 10 Institutions	118.5	22.4	203.5	48.5	368.9	51.8
Next 10 Institutions	49.2	9.3	40.4	9.6	68.8	9.7
All other Institutions	360.2	68.3	175.6	41.9	274.7	38.5
No. of colleges and universities reporting	1,741		1,871		1,940	

referred, which occurred in the late 1940s and early 1950s, might be cited as evidence of a revolutionary new concern of the United States Government with higher education. The passage of the National Defense Education Act in 1958 provided unmistakable evidence of a national concern. And

that this is a continuing phenomenon of our time is clear
from the legislation passed in December 1963 that I have
already mentioned, and the provisions made at the same
time for the expansion of the role of the Federal government in the support of vocational education.[1]

I shall end this chapter by anticipating to some extent
my discussion of education beyond the high school in
Chapter 3. I conclude that the impact of the educational
revolution is such that we must pay more attention to the
way our colleges and universities are chartered and our
public institutions supported. In some states the transformation of a former teachers college into a state college and later
a university may be a matter of political bargaining in the
state legislature. The expansion of the present institutions
may proceed without rhyme or reason. Only in California
and New York have master plans for the development of
public higher education been adopted.

The responsibility for shaping educational policy in
higher education in this country is shared jointly by the
Congress of the United States, the state legislatures, and the
trustees of private colleges and universities. In most public
discussions the role of the Federal government is placed in
the foreground, and little is said about the state legislatures.
Yet my experiences in the capitals of the sixteen most
populous states (which I visited in connection with my
study of teacher education) convinced me of the sig-

[1] Public Law 88-210 authorizes a new permanent program with appropriation for state vocational education programs amounting to $60 mil-
lion for fiscal year 1964, $118.5 million for fiscal year 1965, $177.5 million
for fiscal year 1966, and $225 million for subsequent fiscal years. Funds
would be allotted among the states on the basis of population groups
and a per-capita-income factor (equalization). The new funds may be
expected for state and local vocational education programs without
categorical limitation under a broadened definition of vocational education to fit individuals for gainful employment, embracing all occupations, including business and office occupations not now covered under
existing law.

nificance of policy making at the state level and the need for evolving some ways of more effective cooperation between the states. Indeed, this experience and my sense of horror at the disarray I found in a number of large and important states have led to the writing of the present volume. Discussions of shaping educational policy to meet the challenge of the educational revolution need to be more realistic. Citizens in most states should be as much concerned with what goes on in the capital of their state as with what goes on in Washington. For those who doubt the validity of this statement I have written Chapters 3 and 4. The prospects for interstate cooperation, the limitations on evolving a nationwide educational policy inherent in our federal structure are discussed in the final chapter. In this same chapter I present my own radical suggestion for the creation of a new kind of national council for educational policy. The need is greatest at the level of higher education, but there are also problems, as I have already suggested, in the public schools. Therefore I ask the reader to consider with me in the next chapter some problems of public school policy which have arisen because of the new times in which we live.

CHAPTER 2

Policy Making for the Public Schools

As I have made evident in the preceding pages, I am convinced that the 1960s call for changes in our ways of shaping educational policy. In this chapter I shall document my contention as far as secondary education is concerned. But first I must set forth a few facts about the structure of the organization of our public schools, comment on the role of private accrediting organizations, and recount a bit of history.

I defy anyone to describe in a few pages the organization of education in the United States. The task is easier if one excludes education beyond the high school and talks only about public schools. Even so, since each of the fifty states is sovereign in educational matters, nationwide generalizations are hard to find. With the exception of Alaska and Hawaii, all states have highly decentralized public school systems, with a considerable degree of authority delegated to the local school boards. The legislature is the ultimate source of authority, of course, subject to the provisions of the state constitution and the Constitution of the United States. In almost all states, the legislature has created a lay board to supervise and to some degree control what goes on in the many largely independent school systems. A chief state school officer, elected or appointed, usually works closely with the lay board (often called the state board) and may or may not be directly responsible to it. A generation or two ago, in the then forty-eight states with a decentralized system, the financing of the local schools was largely dependent on real estate taxes. In the last thirty or forty years, local school districts have become more and more dependent on the allocation of state funds. The vast variations among the states as regards the ratio of local to state funds now dispersed for the support of the public schools are illustrated by the following figures: The national average for *local* support is somewhat over 50 per cent, but the percentage is as low as 13 in Delaware and not above 30 in some half dozen states; it is as high as 88 in New Hampshire and over 75 in several other states.

As the inadequacy of the local real estate tax for the support of adequate public schools has become more and more apparent, the importance of state educational officials and a state board has become increasingly clear. As a consequence, members of state legislatures have concerned themselves increasingly with appropriations of state funds for elementary and secondary public schools. This growing concern of state officials with public school financing naturally requires these same officials to direct their attention to such matters as teachers salaries, pension rights, and conditions of employment; and these developments, in turn, have made it imperative that public school personnel be represented at the state capital. Thus voluntary state associations of public school teachers and administrators have grown in size and influence to a point where in all the most populous states they maintain offices and considerable staffs not far distant from the state house. Indeed, in many if not all states, the permanent officials of the state teachers association, together with the officials of the organization of school superintendents, exert considerable influence upon the actions of the legislature and decisions of the state boards. Since the state teachers associations are affiliated with the N E A (National Education Association) and the school superintendents are usually members of the American Association of School Administrators, these two national societies through their meetings and publications exercise a powerful nationwide influence on the policy of the public schools. These two organizations finance the Educational Policies Commission to which I referred in the last chapter, and they appoint its members.

In this quick sketch of the official and unofficial organizations which have determined public school policy in the past, I have left out a number of other important voluntary associations at both the state and national level. The National Association of Secondary-School Principals, for example, has played an important role and has by no means always agreed with the other organizations affiliated with the N E A. Indeed, more than one critic of the establishment has attributed to the N E A a coherence in structure and a unanimity among its constituent segments which are often lacking. Coherence and adherence to a strict party line are to be found at the state level more than at the national level. This fact will become apparent as I proceed with this exposition.

Those who are devoting their lives as teachers or administrators to the welfare of the public schools refer to themselves very often as the professional educators, and the officers of the N E A and its committees and affiliates claim to be the spokesmen for the profession. Without entering into a pointless argument about whether or not schoolteaching is a profession, it is important to remember that college and university professors are also educators.

When pressed, the spokesmen for the public school people will admit that the educational profession includes all professors as well as all schoolteachers, yet in practice only one group of professors, namely the professors of education, is in close contact with those who describe themselves as professional educators.

Now no one can maintain that the public school people have neglected the problems of the schools in favor of the welfare of the individual teacher. To be sure, the question of teacher salaries and conditions of employment has not been overlooked. On the contrary, quite properly, the welfare of the teacher has been constantly called to the attention of state legislators, state officials, and the general public. But the welfare of teachers is not their *only* concern; and moreover, it can well be argued that adequate salaries, reasonably small classes, and other favorable conditions for teachers are directly related to the quality of the work each teacher can perform and thus to the problems of the public schools. With such considerations in mind, at the national level the N E A has for years endeavored, so far in vain, to increase the educational financial resources of each state by massive Federal grants for the public schools.

Shortly before World War I, the N E A appointed a Commission on the Reorganization of Secondary Education. The composition of this commission and the reviewing committees showed the entry in force of the establishment. In the late nineteenth century, the college presidents and private school teachers had had much to say about the relation of school to college. By contrast, the Commission on the Reorganization of Secondary Education was made up largely of public school people and professors of education. The commission's report, printed in 1918 (by the U. S. Bureau of Education), was entitled *Cardinal Principles of Secondary Education.* Together with the reports of seven committees dealing with special topics, this document was taken as the starting point for almost all forward-looking reforms in public high schools for forty years. The opening section carried the title "The Need for Reorganization." The point of view of the authors, which was at that time revolutionary, is revealed by the following quotations:

> The character of the secondary-school population has been modified by the entrance of large numbers of pupils of widely varying capacities, aptitudes, social heredity, and destinies in life. Further, the broadening of the scope of secondary education has brought to the school many pupils who do not complete the full course but leave at various stages of advancement. . . . Education in a democracy, both within and without the school, should develop in each individual the knowledge, interests, ideals, habits and powers whereby he will find his place and use this place to shape both himself and society towards nobler ends.

One of the most significant of the recommendations was that secondary schools admit and provide *suitable instruction* for all pupils who are *in any respect* so mature that they would derive more benefit from the secondary school than from the elementary school. This recommendation, together with the demand for a broader curriculum within the comprehensive high school (which was specifically endorsed), set the unique pattern for American public secondary education which, by the late 1920s, was almost taken for granted throughout the United States. This pattern contrasted sharply with the British and European pattern, which provided selective academic pre-university schools for only a relatively small fraction of their youth, and ended the formal education of all the others at age 14 or 15.

There can be no doubt of the influence of those men and women who wrote the *Cardinal Principles* and who were active in committees in the 1920s and 1930s. Through national, state, and local meetings, through books and articles in educational journals, and above all, through teachings in university schools of education, these people dedicated to public education did in fact shape educational policy for several decades. A historian reviewing the changes in American education in this century (as Professor Cremin has in his excellent book *The Transformation of the School*) readily identifies forces outside the profession which influenced what the professionals themselves advocated. They were far from operating in a vacuum. Within the committees and at the meetings the voices of the superintendents and the school principals were heeded. And these administrators were in constant touch with public opinion. Indeed, this fact, a consequence of our highly decentralized structure, has been a determining factor in our educational history.

Any idea that the professors of education sat in an ivory tower and, accepting the ideas of John Dewey, proceeded to force these ideas on an unwilling public by means of a set of accomplices in the schools is utter nonsense. What the public school people did from the end of World War I until World War II was to start with a very few premises and then develop policy to correspond to the current mood of the American people. The few premises themselves corresponded to the assumptions of the American public fifty years ago. These were (1) free schools for all youth, (2) no differentiation in school organization which seemed to be antidemocratic, (3) heavy emphasis on group activities which also interested adults as parents and spectators (team sports, music, marching bands), and (4) central focus on producing an upright, good citizen, tolerant, fair, committed to honest representative government and "democracy as a way of life."

Even within the framework provided by these few assumptions there was a wide range for changing public school policy in response to public opinion. And the record shows how such changes occurred.

A review of the publications of the Educational Policies Commission illustrates what I have in mind. This organization, appointed by the N E A and the American Association of School Administrators in 1937, has published over a hundred pamphlets and books. The topics reveal the swing of the educational pendulum as the concern of the educators shifted from the depression year, and the fears of a dictator (on the Hitler and Mussolini model), to war, to peace, to new emphasis on education of the gifted, and finally to education of the disadvantaged. The document written for the commission in 1937 by Prof. Charles A. Beard bears the imprint of the worries of American society in the uncertain years of depression. Not only were there vast numbers of unemployed, but many people were questioning the whole structure of society. Hitler and Mussolini had apparently restored material property to their nations; Russia under Stalin was in many eyes not a too unattractive model for the future. Only those of my readers who recall those days can understand Beard's book, which on the first page declares:

> Since the outbreak of the World War in 1914, American society has faced disconcerting issues of life at home and abroad, has experienced storms of passion, and encountered the vicissitudes of a profound economic dislocation. The human and economic destruction of the war itself, the ensuing overthrow of governments and social systems in Europe, the collapse of prosperity in the United States, and the jars of the depression have shaken American thought and practice from center to circumference.

The uncertainty of the 1930s is reflected in the section headed "The Assurance of Democratic Society No Longer Taken for Granted." In the text Beard states that:

> . . . from 1870 to 1920 education took for granted the future of democratic society and, perhaps to a less extent, the eternal validity of the theory that both individual prosperity and social security were to be automatically assured by the free application of talents to personal ends. Now the future of democratic society is challenged, not only in Europe and Asia,

but in quarters by no means obscure or negligible in the United States. . . . Once more, as in the early days of the Republic, the terms, conditions, and methods appropriate to the maintenance of democratic society swing into the center of educational interest.

The swing to which Beard referred dominated much of the curriculum planning of the public schools in all the states in the Union. The emphasis on education for citizenship, for understanding the ways of democracy, for cooperation among individuals, of developing social attitudes in a new industrial society—all these matters were written about and discussed in endless meetings during the 1930s and well into the 1940s.

To be sure, not all the changes advocated by the Educational Policies Commission have proved to be successful. That is to say they have not all found widespread approval even though they represented the "best thinking" of the leaders in the establishment. For example, in *Education for ALL American Youth,* the program suggested for grades 10 through 12 provided for a third of a student's time to be known as "Common Learnings." Such a course, it was stated, was to be "planned to help sudents grow in competence as citizens of the community and the nation; in understanding of economic processes and of their roles as producers and consumers; in cooperative living in family, schools and community; in appreciation of literature and the arts; and in the use of the English language." Guidance of individual students was to be a chief responsibility of "Common Learnings" teachers.

In answer to the question what is meant by the words "Common Learnings," the authors (and I was one of them) stated that "this course consists of learning experience which *everyone* needs to have, regardless of what occupation he may expect to follow or where he may happen to live." To quote further from the same document, it was declared that "under the proposed comprehensive course, students can better understand the relations between the different things they are learning." English language, literature, history, and science would certainly be found among the "Common Learnings," the reader is assured, "though possibly in unaccustomed settings." Since in grades 11 and 12 an even greater amount of time (half of the day) is set aside for elective courses, the belief was expressed that there need be no fear of "an end to the systematic study of bodies of knowledge, such as science, mathematics, history, and languages . . . and there would be ample time in the total school program for any student who wished to do so to complete all the courses in subject fields required for admission to college or university. . . ."

The interest in describing a common core of studies for the high school which was reflected in *Education for All American Youth* coincided with a widespread interest in "general education" at the college level. No one can today find more than a trace of a "Common Learnings" in the high schools; furthermore general education programs at the college level are not as flourishing as they were a decade ago. In this case those within the educational establishment who were trying to shape policy were not successful for a number of reasons, which I think can be summed up by saying the reforms proposed were too difficult to realize and never captured the public imagination (as did for example the expansion of athletics and public musical performances).

One change which was early brought about by the educational reformers grouped under the N E A banner was the destruction of the foreign language program in the public schools. Here the public was in tune with what the public school people demanded. Or one can say the establishment was merely responding to the public demands (I have no intention of discussing such complicated cause and effect formulations). The fact is that teachers of Latin and Greek were fighting a rear-guard action a generation before World War I, even at the college level. Their arguments were becoming weaker and weaker and finding less and less support from the public. (The same phenomenon is occurring today in Great Britain and Europe.) The modern foreign language teachers were bound by the traditions of treating a language as something to be read and rarely spoken. The arguments in support of their activities met with little response during the period of isolationism between the two World Wars. What had been four-year programs of the study of either Latin or French or German (or often two of the three) in the high schools of 1900–1910 had degenerated to a program of two years of Latin and two years of French or Spanish by the 1940s. Such were the foreign language programs which I found when I visited the high schools in 1958. No one claimed that those who elected such a course of study could either read or write or speak the foreign language on graduation. To be sure, some of the private colleges still continued to require the study of a foreign language of candidates for admission, but the requirement (or recommendations) of only two years seemed to give approval to a situation so bad as to be almost ludicrous.

World War II, the new United States international position, the troops overseas, and the airplane have altered radically the public mood. Furthermore, the new direct method of teaching a modern language, coupled with the use of tape recorders to enable pupils to hear a language well pronounced and also, if desired, to record their own attempts and play them back, have revolutionized language teaching in institutions. Such steps corresponded to the revolution in American public opinion, which had come to demand that a pupil learn a modern foreign language.

What is now going on at a rapid rate in the field of language instruction is an illustration of what I referred to in the last chapter. The public school people after World War II started to sense the significance of worldwide changes and the changed mood of the American public.

Their position became more and more defensive. This was largely a quite understandable reaction to harsh unfair criticism which appeared to come in part from those intent on undermining public confidence in the public school system. But I need not repeat here what I have already said; namely, that leaving aside all criticism of the failure of the establishment and its friends (among whom I count myself) to respond to the needs of the 1950s, the time has come for a new look at shaping educational policy. Make a list of ten problems now facing our public schools without attempting to place them in order of priority. Recall the facts of the educational revolution I outlined in the last chapter, and then see how many fall outside of the interest and competence of the establishment.

My list would be as follows:

1. The reform of instructional methods and materials including the new developments in foreign language instruction in the lower grades and the new courses in physics, chemistry, mathematics, and biology

2. The advanced placement program

3. The improvement in the instruction in English composition

4. The introduction of new techniques including T.V. and programmed instruction

5. The recruiting of more intellectually able young people into the teaching profession

6. The education of students of limited ability in the high school

7. Vocational education

8. Teaching reading to the children of disadvantaged families

9. The slum schools

10. Segregated schools

The first five items involve changes which were not initiated by the establishment and some of which have been resisted by the Old Guard. The first two require active leadership by subject matter professors, not professors of education.

The last item is political; the establishment has never dared tackle it. Today there are separate teacher training institutions in the South and separate teacher organizations. The layman and the college professor here must be brought into the picture. But more of this later.

Items 1 and 2 may be considered together. What was basic to both developments was the growing awareness that as our public high schools were operating, the intellectually able youth were not being sufficiently challenged. The content of courses which in the 1930s had been sneered at as "old fashioned academic courses" was in fact old-fashioned. But left to themselves, it is now clear that, with few exceptions, those who had been shaping policy would not have brought about the required reforms. The development of a new approach to high school physics started by Professor Zacharias of the Massachusetts Institute of Technology in the late 1950s started a chain reaction of significant developments. New approaches to high school chemistry and biology followed. Drastic reforms in school mathematics were being pushed at about the same time by several groups, and the Modern Language Association was introducing the direct method and urging an early start on studying a modern language. None of these developments was taken up with enthusiasm by those who had been determining policy; but, what is more important, *these and similar reforms can not now be discussed or planned without the participation of subject matter professors.*

The case is particularly clear in considering the advanced placement program (item 2). And a consideration of this significant phase of the educational revolution leads me to consider the way the establishment has developed organizations to enforce some of its decisions. I refer to the regional accrediting associations. Of the voluntary accrediting agencies, the most powerful is the North Central

Association. Essentially an association of secondary schools and colleges (private and public), it exercises enormous powers through the state committees. For example, for a high school or a private secondary school to be accredited, the school must conform to many requirements. These include specifications as to the education of the teachers (with which I have quarreled elsewhere). In theory, schools and colleges must stand the scrutiny of a visiting team in order to be accredited. In practice, only a few schools and colleges which are scandalously inferior are refused accreditation. The concept of a comprehensive high school and a comprehensive college as well as a tolerance for low academic standards are all part of the premises of the association and correspond to the folkways of the American public.

I do not wish to attempt to draw up a balance sheet of the advantages and disadvantages which have accrued to our society by the operation of the regional accrediting associations. I have elsewhere expressed my views about the role of an accrediting association in the state certification of teachers. Even the most devastating critics would have to admit that, as far as high schools and four-year colleges were concerned, a certain degree of order has resulted from the activities of the regional associations. (Few laymen realize how powerful has been the North Central Association.) However, as one consequence of the educational revolution, their power is now diminishing at least in some states; the only sanction which can be employed is the threat to remove the high school from the accredited list. Such a removal today would not be as significant as it would have been twenty years ago, when few colleges would have been ready to admit a graduate of a "discredited" school. Now the widespread use of aptitude and achievement tests administered by the College Entrance Examination Board has made the issue of whether or not an applicant has attended an accredited school of relatively little significance. An applicant with high scores on the tests and a good school record is likely to be accepted by the most selective colleges, even if the school he attended has been removed from the accredited list by the North Central Association.

The statement of major policies of the North Central Association (note the use of the word "policies") lays down detailed specifications. The concept of the comprehensive high school as it had developed between the two World Wars is taken as complete and never to be altered. There is no emphasis on the new movement to challenge an even greater number of able students, to encourage the study of mathematics, to introduce a sensible foreign language program, to introduce ways of assessing whether the guidance people are really guiding everyone into as wide and deep an academic program as possible. There is no evidence of interest in the advanced placement program.

In short, the regional accrediting associations are not in a position to plan a modern high school curriculum for the academically talented nor to come to grips with the problems of the acceleration of the more able students either by offering Freshman college work in the 12th grade or by earlier entry to college. I venture the opinion, therefore, that the era of nationwide school policy planning by unofficial agencies reflecting only the opinions of the establishment is drawing to a close. As an interstate planning agency for the public schools, the network of N E A - affiliated state organizations is coming to be less and less effective; as a method of enforcement, the regional accrediting agencies are rapidly losing ground.

I must emphasize that the regional accrediting associations are in fact regional. There has never been an attempt to merge them into one national accrediting agency comparable to the North Central Association. So in a sense, there is no nationwide machinery for the implementation of

Table 4. Statistics on 16 Most Populous States*

	A	B	C	D	E	F	G
California	620	111.2%	9.8%	$7,050	86.4%	$516	$42.72
Florida	218	98.6	6.7	5,450	62.9	347	13.37
Georgia	398	22.6	3.0	4,637	51.8	298	13.34
Illinois	131	59.4	21.9	6,360	84.5	526	15.79
Indiana	32	45.6	11.3	6,150	74.1	405	28.17
Massachusetts	208	48.7	22.2	6,075	68.2	465	5.88
Michigan	163	50.6	15.5	6,444	78.4	447	30.00
Missouri	122	27.1	15.8	5,289	73.0	405	10.69
New Jersey	222	53.6	21.1	6,308	78.8	556	8.73
New York	706	38.0	22.6	6,950	74.1	645	10.77
North Carolina	180	25.0	1.4	4,975	57.4	297	15.86
Ohio	203	59.7	14.8	5,750	72.4	422	16.05
Pennsylvania	290	23.8	23.5	5,660	78.0	464	7.63
Texas	279	51.7	6.5	5,300	60.6	379	18.18
Virginia	169	41.7	6.4	4,950	51.9	335	14.83
Wisconsin	59	44.2	25.8	5,650	92.3	467	20.86
National Average	137	44.6%	13.6%	$5,735	70.6%	$432	$19.50

A: Size of State Department of Education Professional Staff July, 1960.
B: Percentage of Change in Public Elementary and Secondary School Enrollments, 1952–53 to 1962–63.
C: Nonpublic School Enrollment as Per Cent of Total Enrollment in Elementary and Secondary Schools, 1959–60.
D: Estimated Average Salaries of Classroom Teachers in Public Schools, 1962–63.
E: High School Graduates in 1962 as Per Cent of Eighth Grade Enrollment in 1957–58.
F: Estimated Current Expenditure for Public Elementary and Secondary Schools per Pupil in A D A (Average Daily Attendance), 1962–63.
G: Expenditures for State Institutions of Higher Education per Capita of Population, 1961.

* Source for all columns except column A: Rankings of the States, 1963, Research Division, National Education Association.
   Source for column A: U. S. Department of Health, Education, and Welfare, Office of Education.

what might be a consensus of the educational establishment nationally. I must further emphasize that no other regional association has exercised such powers as those of the North Central Association. And it is surely significant that with few exceptions the states with the weakest state departments of education (of the sixteen most populous states) are those in the region covered by the North Central Association. This fact is demonstrated by the first column of Table 4, if one bears in mind that of the sixteen states the following fall within the jurisdiction of the North Central Association: Illinois, Indiana, Missouri, Ohio, Wisconsin. In none of the other of the sixteen states do state committees of a regional accrediting agency perform the functions of the state committees (completely unofficial, remember) of Illinois, Indiana, Missouri, Ohio, and Wisconsin.

Some readers may take a far more negative view of the record made by the public school people than I do. They may be in favor of eliminating their influence. Any such proposal, I submit, is unwise in theory and impractical. What is needed, according to my view, is to discredit the accrediting agencies, increase the effectiveness of the state educational authorities, and see to it that the state brings about an integration of the views of the state teacher association, the professors of education, the academic professors, and the laymen. The state school board association should be urged to work more closely with the professional educators than is usual in most states. The year-by-year battle between the state taxpayers association and the professionals should give place to a more rational though vigorous exchange of views looking forward to long-range planning. All this must center on the state capital primarily. As to how the state-by-state plans may be developed into a nationwide policy, I shall have more to say later. In most states what is required is for those interested in improving education to make their views heard at the state capital, not to get the legislature to enact laws dealing with specific issues (this is just what ought *not* to happen), but in order to have a strong department of education. What is needed are strong state boards of education, a first-class chief state school officer, a well-organized state staff, and good support from the legislature.

As an example of what can be accomplished by a state to help the public schools keep pace with the educational revolution consider what has happened in New York. In 1960 an account for laymen of the result of educational experiments was prepared for the state authorities and published in book form as *Schools of Tomorrow—TO-DAY!* In December 1961, the Board of Regents (equivalent to a state board of educators) published a 100-page pamphlet entitled *Organizing New York State for Educational Change.* In addition the state published the commissioner's 1961 Catalog of Educational Change (the chief state school officer in New York is the commissioner of education). In this catalog each local school board superintendent or high school principal can find a brief account of hundreds of new programs. What is even more important, the catalog gives the names and addresses of those to whom one may write for further information. No one could ask for a better response from a state system faced with the impact of the American phase of the educational revolution, unless indeed, one were prepared to give the state authorities the power to *mandate* change, or in other words to establish a close state control of the curricula.

In urging each state to organize itself so that it can bring about a cooperative enterprise in policy formation, I admit I am indulging in optimistic hopes. As I shall show in Chapter 4, New York is so far an exception. But that does not mean other states could not follow its example. To do so a state requires a well-financed, well-staffed state department of education and a tradition in which the public school people do not control the state educational machinery. As evidence of the independence of New York State authorities, I may cite the fact that New York still continues to give statewide regents examinations in the schools, although nearly every member of the establishment with whom I have talked has been in favor of their abolition

(I have never taken a position on this issue since the pros and cons seem so nearly balanced). Now it is possible to have a relatively strong state department of education but have it completely in the hands of the establishment. Such is the case in New Jersey, for example. But this is not a situation I would advocate. In urging that the state step in to take the place of such accrediting agencies as the North Central, I have in mind New York as an example.

More often than not the state public school leaders (the state establishment, if you will) have worked against the development of a strong state department, for the obvious reason that they feared they could not control it. The old "bogey" of political patronage has been used as the chief argument as to why the professionals (meaning only the teachers, administrators, and professors of education) should have full sway. There may be a few states where this fear of politicians may be justified, but the answer lies not in excluding state officials altogether, but in having a strong nonpolitical alignment of the forces of *all* educators and laymen.

However, to be frank about the difficulties that must be faced, let me recount what I have seen and heard in the two states of Indiana and Illinois. In both states the chief state school officer is elected. In both states the state education departments, though possessing considerable formal authority, are capable of little more than the performance of routine duties. In Indiana the state superintendent is elected on partisan ballot every two years; at least one of the state's two major parties has shown relatively little interest in the office and it has on occasion been used as a dumping ground for individuals who were held in low repute by leading party dignitaries. In other words, the state superintendent in Indiana is a political official subject to political pressures. party dignitaries. In other words, the state superintendent in Indiana is a political official subject to political pressures.

The superintendent's staff does not have civil service status, with the obvious result that it is difficult to recruit and retain high-quality people.

Indiana's State Board of Education, which consists of three six-member commissions, dealing with different phases of education, the members of each of which are appointed by the governor, also leaves much to be desired. As presently constituted, the Indiana Board of Education is overwhelmingly controlled by what I have referred to as the educational establishment. As one informant stated, "We have a situation in Indiana in which the lay people do not set policy or control education. Public policy is made almost exclusively by a vested-interest group, the professional educators."

The present administrative setup in Indiana has been backed by an alert and very powerful organized group, the Indiana State Teachers Association. The organization is led by its executive secretary, Robert Wyatt, who is regarded as one of the state's most powerful lobbyists. In fact, the special imprint this organization has made on the state's education policy can be credited to the extraordinary zeal with which Mr. Wyatt has presented public school needs to the governor and the state legislature.

The I S T A readily admits that the state's educational structure is weak, and with the department weak, the association is able to fill the power vacuum. That is, if Indiana were to create an entirely lay board which appointed the chief state school officer, it would be reasonable to assume that the association's influence would be less pervasive. Such changes have been recommended more than once in Indiana, but all such efforts have encountered the vigorous opposition of the I S T A. To me, this seems most unfortunate.

The educational machinery in Illinois judged by the standards of some of the other more populous states is also seriously defective. The state superintendent, like his

Indiana counterpart, is elected on a partisan ballot. His nomination and election are inextricably interwoven with the politics of the state. A candidate for the office is heavily dependent on the party machinery to deliver the necessary votes, though occasionally a particular personality may generate wide appeal on other grounds. Illinois is also a patronage state, and therefore the Illinois Office of Education does not have the continuity found in "civil service" states such as New York or Ohio. The professional personnel of the office do not survive election after election; their tenure depends on who wins, although there has been a tendency in recent years to retain a few professional staff members. The office, again like that of Indiana, has difficulty in recruiting competent people. The clerical personnel are all on a patronage basis; their names are drawn from the "pool" of the state central committee of the incumbent party.

The state superintendent is directly responsible to the electorate, since Illinois has no state board of education. The state has its own special and unique machinery to fill the void left by the absence of a state board. The agency is a legislative-executive advisory committee called the Illinois School Problems Commission. The state superintendent serves as ex-officio member; the other members are appointed by the governor and the state legislature.

The School Problems Commission has been a highly effective agency in Illinois politics.* It has been able to push through much badly needed legislation concerning school finance and local district reorganization. The commission has in addition made a number of penetrating analyses of public school needs. However, it seems to me that the commission is not an acceptable substitute for a full-time administrative agency, mainly because it confines its activities largely to questions of finance and school district reorganization. It *does not* deal with such important

* Masters, Nicholas A.; Robert S. Salisbury; and Thomas H. Eliot: *State Politics and the Public Schools.* Alfred A. Knopf, 1964, Chapter 3.

questions as curriculum, textbook selection, and related educational policies.

Let us face frankly the fact that the state organization of teachers and their allies may in some states favor an elected chief state school officer because such an officer will be in a relatively weak position. The weaker the state officialdom, the more powerful the unofficial bodies which lobby each session of the legislature in favor of the teachers and the welfare of the public schools.

Indiana is a classic example of a situation which, to my mind, serves as a model of a less than satisfactory way of organizing the state for public education. Education in Illinois shows that an elected chief state school officer running on a partisan ticket is under compulsion when elected to see to it that his chief associates and helpers are of the same party. "To the victor belongs the spoils" is a slogan that, while it is realistic about American politics, should have as little applicability as possible in public education. The main objection to an elected chief state school officer is that discussion of education issues in a political campaign easily becomes emotional and irrational. Furthermore, an elected chief state school officer is either surrounded by a staff protected by civil service regulations (which makes it difficult for him to operate effectively), or his office is composed of patronage appointees.

The last point raises a most important theme, which runs through all discussions of representative government. A permanent staff of experts is, today, needed in all branches of government in a free society. Yet how can the people be protected against the abuse of power by the experts now to be labeled as bureaucrats? To venture opinion about the Federal government would lead me too far afield, but the problem exists in Washington, as we all are well aware. As far as state educational activities are concerned, it seems to me a clear case can be made for having a few full-time officials responsible directly or indirectly to the elected representatives. These people are expendable, as is a college president. Once the legislature has lost confidence in them, their usefulness is at an end. A state board composed of laymen appointed for long terms by the governor is a common device. *Such a board, in my opinion, should then have the power to appoint and remove the chief state school officer as a board of trustees has the same power as regards the president of the state university.*

The formal structure of state educational machinery poses a serious problem in only some of the states, those in which the chief state school officer is an *elected* official and those in which there is no responsible lay board. I should advocate strongly a lay board which appoints the superintendent. Beyond this I leave it to the specialists on organization to tinker with the administrative machinery.

The major weakness of all of the state departments of education I have encountered, with perhaps one or two exceptions, is that they are too much a part of the educational establishment. That is, I found many of these agencies, not unlike the regulatory commissions at the Federal level, to be little more than the "willing tools" of the interests and clientele, particularly the education association. In more than one state I heard highly placed educational and political officials claim that state departments of education "follow a party line" or "reflect the public school mentality." These terms were used in a derogatory sense. A grave shortcoming of our educational leadership at the state level, in my opinion, is often its unwillingness or incapacity to respond to forces outside the establishment. These agencies seldom solicit the opinions of educational experts or critics who are not associated with public schools or professional education, and in those rare instances when they do ask the advice of "outside" experts, I suspect it is largely for symbolic purposes. Too often, educational leadership at the state level—official and un-official—has been open to the charge that it was unwilling to examine public school needs critically.

I found a great reluctance on the part of some state education departments to concern themselves with the special problems of school districts in highly urbanized areas. I found insufficient efforts in some states toward more sensible organization of our public schools. To be sure, great accomplishments have been made toward a more efficient organization of our public schools and the reduction of the number of small high schools. But now that the general public concern with quality education that was generated by the launching of the first Soviet sputnik has subsided somewhat, it seems that inertia has set in, and state departments have become once again overly sensitive to the political consequences of efforts to overhaul the existing pattern of school district organization.

As between educational policy making within a state by the establishment (as in Indiana) or by a strong department of education (as in New York), there is no question of choice to my mind. I am convinced that the future welfare of our public schools will be promoted by the organization of excellent state departments of education, granted the framework I have already recommended. A powerful chief state school officer responsible to a high-quality lay board of education can provide the type of state leadership for the schools which the times demand. The publications issued by the Board of Regents of New York State to which I earlier referred should be examined by all who may question both my judgment and my optimism as to the possibility of effective official leadership at the state level.

The Education of·the Negro

I now turn to the tenth problem on my list, segregated schools. I hardly need point out that until recently all concerned with shaping policy for elementary and secondary education have either ignored the subject of Negro education or accepted completely segregated schools as a matter of course. No state official until very recently has even admitted the existence of a problem. School people and professors, with very few exceptions, have written about American education without even describing the different ways in which children of Negro families have been offered educational opportunities, depending largely on the proportion of such families in the school district. We have talked about our public school system and how it responds to and is conditioned by all types of groups and social classes *except* the Negro.

Consider, for example, how all of us who have written in praise of the comprehensive high school have turned our backs on the obvious exception to the definition of such a school. A comprehensive high school is a school in which *all* the youth of an area attend the same school, or so we have often said. Such a school is an American invention. It has been attacked because youth with different abilities, interests, and ambitions are all enrolled in one and the same school; the claim has been made that the intellectually more able should attend separate academic high schools and those who want practical courses should attend vocational high schools. (In a few Eastern cities such a system is in partial operation.) The comprehensive high school has been defended on social and political grounds as an instrument of democracy, a way of mitigating the social stratification of society. Such has always been my argument. But neither I nor anyone else, as far as I am aware, has underlined the fact that in the former Confederate States no comprehensive high schools have ever existed. When I undertook to study the comprehensive high school in 1957, I knew full well there were no truly comprehensive schools in a number of Southern states. I was tempted to exclude these states from my study and say frankly why. But I did not do so. I visited schools in states where at the most there has been only token integration since the Supreme Court decision. And I said not a word to indicate that certain schools I visited were comprehensive only in so far as white youth were concerned.

The members of the establishment have been as silent as any of us as to the limitation on the concept of the comprehensive high school as an instrument of democracy. There was no reference to the situation in the South in the *Cardinal Principles,* nor in *Education for All American Youth* (which went through many editions) though both documents vigorously supported the idea of the comprehensive school. Furthermore, the state organizations of teachers in the former Confederate States have developed on the tacit assumption that the schools were segregated and would remain segregated for the foreseeable future. Only within the last few years have voices been raised within the N E A to question the complete separation of Negro and white teachers in professional organizations. Not even a mixed administrative group tries to develop a joint policy at the state capitals in the former Confederate States.

In all the discussions of Negro education that have appeared in the last ten years very little reference has been made to the education of teachers in the Southern states. I was not fully aware of the complete separation of Negro and white teachers in these states until I visited Virginia, Georgia, Florida, North Carolina, and Texas in connection with my study of the education of American teachers. We spent a considerable amount of time visiting completely segregated Negro colleges of education or Negro liberal arts colleges from which a high percentage of the graduates became teachers. I had not realized to what a degree becoming a teacher in an all-Negro school or college was one of the very few opportunities for intellectual employment open to those whose skins were not white. The state authorities had provided excellent physical facilities for the most part, at least in the state colleges I visited. The professors were dedicated educators keenly alive to the implication of the educational revolution. But the human limitation because of the nature of the student body was discouraging. Boys and girls who had lived all their lives in a completely segregated small community in a society dominated by white people and had graduated from a segregated Negro high school were ill prepared to undertake college work. The level of reading and competence in mathematics, for example, of a freshman in the few instances I explored was far below that of what one would expect in even the least selective of the state universities in the North and West. The influence of the socio-economic situation, the lack of family and community interest in reading books, magazines, and even papers, and above all the blocks to ambition, a consequence of the segregated policy of society, had so handicapped these youngsters from the start that only a very few could reach the levels of accomplishment in academic subjects expected of students in a nonsegregated college. These few usually went North or West to a university to do graduate work. The rest were graduated as teachers for the Negro elementary and secondary schools. They returned with as much training as conscientious professors could provide but without the kind of comprehension of many fields of learning which I, for one, would specify for all teachers. Through no fault of any one individual, but as a consequence of the system, these less-than-satisfactory teachers returned to the far-less-than-satisfactory school. The vicious wheel continued to revolve.

Statistics are available that would make more vivid the unpleasant facts I have just outlined. There is no need to underline the tragedy of Negro education in a segregated state. It is sufficient if the kind of information I have just given is realized both North and South. For too long discussion has been silenced by all educators and all state teachers organizations, Negro and white alike. The reader will bear in mind I have been writing about the education of the Negro in the segregated states. And that such states exist and are different from the other states is a fact that needs underlining in any rational discussion of what is the most serious political-educational problem facing the United States today.

I am well aware that in recent years the leaders in the movement to create something like equal opportunities for Negroes have tended to blur the distinction between the Negro schools in segregated states and the all-Negro schools in states where some mixed schools do in fact exist. I venture to think that for the long-run solution of the problem this tendency is a mistake, because what is needed to solve the general problem—admittedly a national problem—of adequate education for the Negro is a state-by-state analysis and a state-by-state decision.

In terms of social prejudice, in terms of justice to an individual, in terms of social consequences the completely Negro school in a Northern or Western state may be as bad as a segregated school in a segregated state. But the approach to a long-range eradication of the two evils must depend on a realistic analysis of the factors involved, and they are as different as the histories of the two types of segregated schools. In the practically completely segregated Southern states, in which there are separate Negro and white state teachers associations, there have never been any mixed schools. In the states in which there are today what are called *de facto* segregated schools, all-Negro schools are a relatively recent development. In these states there are mixed schools and school systems with mixed staffs. The state authorities, with perhaps some exceptions, have declared that the schools should be open to all irrespective of color. Let us consider what is needed in *such* states to get forward with a mitigation of the present almost unbearable situation.

The first matter to be attended to is the formulation of

a *state* policy. The issue should be transferred from the local level and the courts as far as possible. The state, by legislative resolution or by the action of a powerful and respected *state board, should declare that the public schools as far as possible should be comprehensive schools.* The chief state school officer should be directed to proceed to report what steps, however radical, would be required to reduce to a minimum the number of noncomprehensive schools, both elementary and secondary. A moment's consideration makes it plain that whether or not a given school is mixed or essentially all-Negro depends on its neighborhood. A recognition of this basic fact, of course, has led in the past to the gerrymandering of attendance lines within a district by some local boards so that in fact some schools would be all-white, others all-Negro. Looked at from the point of view of those who wish to have the maximum number of truly comprehensive schools (i.e., mixed schools), a radical redistricting in some sections of some states would be highly desirable. It could change the balance of Negro and white families in many school districts.

Such a measure as the redrawing of district lines to insure a mixed population within each district is perhaps too radical to be practical, but the possibility should be faced squarely nonetheless. There are areas around many of the large cities in New York, Massachusetts, Connecticut, New Jersey, Illinois, and Missouri, to name but a few examples, where if one could start fresh in creating autonomous school districts, some completely white districts could disappear. There would still be other areas within the state where there were no Negro families and redistricting such areas to create mixed schools would be impossible.

Of course, any redistricting must carry with it proposals for financing and managing the schools, and the inherent difficulties are very great. Yet setting forth the consequences of such a radical approach, and also the failure to adopt such a recommendation, would do much to clarify a fundamental issue. For there can be no question that as long as families within a state are free to establish essentially segregated residential areas that may correspond to state-created school districts, it may be impossible to have mixed schools. I conclude therefore that one must recognize that the *power of the state to establish school districts is a fundamental fact that must be brought out into the open, and state policy in regard to the school districts therefore must be examined and clearly stated.*

Such an examination should be made state by state and debated in the legislature eventually. Those who reject the radical proposal to redistrict the state to provide for the maximum number of mixed schools might come up with an alternative state policy. It might be as follows: assuming the present school districts, the state should adopt the principle that every school within a given district should be a mixed school, the composition of which should correspond to the composition of the entire district (in terms of the percentage of Negroes and whites). Of course, the application of this principle would result in a great variety of mixed schools. I can think of some where all the schools would be 90 per cent white and others in which all the schools would be 90 per cent Negro. Yet if one is looking for a statewide principle and is an advocate of as many mixed schools as possible, such a principle has much to recommend it and could be relatively easily enforced by state authorities.

One difficulty with either of the two proposals I have just discussed is that in many areas, pupils would have to be transported some distance. Negro children and white children both would have to take buses, because the residential patterns would rarely correspond to the pattern of the whole district; many present neighborhood schools would have to be transformed. Now the concept of the neighborhood school is almost as dear to most American public school people as the principle of the comprehensive high school. In both cases educational considerations become mixed with political and sociological arguments. *The same kind of arguments are used to support both public neighborhood schools and public comprehensive high schools.* These are the arguments many of us have often used against the use of taxpayers' money to support private schools. The children from different homes should go to school together. Separate schools based on religion or income or social standing of parents are a divisive force in our society.

So the argument goes. But notice how the concept of the neighborhood school emerges: the school's atmosphere feeds back to the families; the mingling of the children from different socio-economic levels affects the spirit of the neighborhood. The community and the school interact together. If every neighborhood were a cross section of the American population, the conflict of goals between neighborhood schools and mixed schools would not exist. As a matter of fact, neighborhoods correspond to residential patterns that reflect differences in the socio-economic level of the families, and in the case of Negroes reflect the prejudices of a vast number of white families. Historically the elementary public school has been a neighborhood school and there are strong arguments for its continuing to be a neighborhood school. These have been presented in a document published by the Educational Policies Commission entitled *Education of the Disadvantaged.*

Yet there can be no doubt that because of the segregated residential patterns in almost all cities and towns in all states, North and South, the neighborhood school is often either 100 per cent white or 100 per cent Negro. In terms of a cross section of the *entire school district*, the neighborhood school is thus often not a comprehensive school. What is to be done about such a situation if the present school districts are to be maintained? This question is critical in the large cities today. My own answer would be, as a last resort after all readjustment of attendance lines had failed to provide enough mixed schools, to be prepared to bus high school students in such numbers and in such a way that each high school would be *as comprehensive* as the total school district. The elementary schools I should leave as neighborhood schools even if many were as a consequence essentially all-Negro. But as I have pointed out in my book *Slums and Suburbs,* I should advocate pouring money into such schools with the hope of overcoming the incredible handicaps under which children in the Negro slum schools now suffer. But my views on this subject are for the purposes of this book neither here nor there. *The point is the state should adopt a clear-cut detailed policy at the highest level.* If drastic district reorganization is out of the question (such as combining slum areas of a city with nearby suburban independent school districts), then the specifications to the school boards about attendance lines, busing pupils, and the composition of the school staffs should be made quite clear.

I have written about the development by public debate of a state policy in the nonsegregated states. I have done so because the problems in these states in theory are easiest to solve. For, theoretically, public opinion in the non-segregated states would be ready to accept some such general principle as "the greater the number of mixed schools, the better." The political resistance in the segregated states presents another problem. Public opinion might well split on a fundamental issue, which I believe would finally come down to accepting the principle of the comprehensive school or abolishing all public schools within the state. Although I shall not pursue this particular problem further, I should point out as a practical matter that if one of the present segregated states were to adopt the principle of the comprehensive school, two important details would have to be examined in full. One would be the gradual integration of the present completely separate teaching staffs, the other the timing of the transformation of the schools in different school districts. The discussion of the various alternatives of resolving the conflict of aims between a comprehensive school and a neighborhood school in the preceding pages would be applicable to the segregated states once the state had accepted the principle of comprehension and worked out a time schedule for its adoption, district by district, over the next twenty years.

To sum up this discussion on policy for our public schools, it seems clear that so far neither the establishment nor the state educational administrative hierarchy has faced up to the problem of segregated schools. The educators alone cannot possibly formulate policy in this area, but they can help. State by state certain basic issues should be faced, state by state a policy should be hammered out, and lay opinion here would be far more important than the views of educators. Superficially an educational issue seems to be at stake. What is really involved, however, is a deep-seated pattern of racial discrimination as expressed in housing and in employment. An educational policy can either reinforce racial prejudice or try to mitigate its evil influence. The comprehensive high school is designed for the latter purpose; alone it cannot solve the basic problem, but each state that sets it up as an ideal and then strives toward it will be moving in the right direction. One cannot expect every state to set up the same timetable, but each state ought to face the issue. What could be done to correlate policy among states on this and other issues I shall consider in the concluding chapter of this book.

CHAPTER 3
Policy Making for Higher Education

In the last chapter I urged that each state exercise as much authority in regard to its public schools as does New York. This means for most states a vast increase in the power of the state vis-à-vis the local boards on the one hand and the professional educators on the other. More than one reader must have felt his gorge rising at the thought of increasing the power of state officials. Indeed, it is just this almost instinctive anti-centralized-government reaction of Americans that has allowed the establishment, through its voluntary accrediting agencies, to capture so large a degree of control over elementary and secondary education. A similar hostility to those in the state capital may be some people's first reaction to my thesis in this chapter, which is that the state should plan more carefully for the development of education beyond the high school. But in this case, the reaction is hardly justified, for the issue is not one of more or less state control, but of the wiser exercise of this control. For public education above the high school has traditionally, with a few exceptions, been a function of the state, not of the local communities.

The states differ markedly in their attempts to provide public facilities for education beyond high school. The differences are largely to be traced to the role of private colleges and universities. In the older states where many private institutions were flourishing as early as the mid-nineteenth century, there was a tendency to regard higher education as the province of private institutions, even at a time when public responsibility for free schools was universally recognized. In the states of Massachusetts, New Jersey, and New York, for example, there were no state-supported universities as late as the 1940s comparable to the state universities of the Middle Western and Far Western states. Even today there is a striking difference in the per capita expenditure for *public* higher education in the nine most populous states as shown below. There are no figures available for private expenditure for higher education. Therefore one has no way of knowing the total sums provided for colleges and universities within each state, but I feel sure that in terms of these totals there would be comparatively little difference among these nine states.

California	$42.72
Michigan	30.60
Indiana	28.70
Wisconsin	20.86
Ohio	16.65
New York	10.77
New Jersey	8.73
Pennsylvania	7.63
Massachusetts	5.88

The Publicly Supported Institutions

Every two years at least the legislature in each state must appropriate large sums of money for public education at all levels. Furthermore, almost without exception, the legislature must consider bills affecting the organization and operation of public schools, colleges, and universities. Ideally one might wish that the entire public educational system of a state from the kindergarten to the graduate schools of the university would be looked at as a whole. But as matters stand today, the legislative actions involving higher education on the one hand and schools on the other rarely overlap. They tend to fall into two categories corresponding to the state agencies responsible for the administration of the state-supported system.

As we have seen, the public schools with all their problems are in general within the jurisdiction of a chief state school officer and a state board of education. The state university (or universities) are usually, like many private colleges and universities, chartered institutions, and the guidelines for their management are set forth in the charter. The state colleges (many of which were originally normal schools) may be under the supervision of the same body that is responsible for the elementary or secondary schools, or they may be subject to the authority of a separate state board or individual boards.

The purpose of the first section of the present chapter is to explore the way policies for public institutions tend to be adopted by state legislatures and their agents. I shall examine some examples to see how the complicated questions of expansion and control of public higher education are often answered with relatively little attention to long-range plans, which should take into account state and national needs.

One of the most conspicuous characteristics of the educational interests at the university and college levels in many states is the lack of consensus among the interests. Genuine political battles have become the normal pattern. These political struggles have no precise boundaries. Public higher education institutions compete with each other and with private institutions; even the resident campuses within the same university compete with each other and with the parent body. The debate between public and private institutions has been conducted primarily on the national level, whereas conflict among public institutions has been most intense within state boundaries. As one writer puts it:

> The real conflict occurs among institutions, often with very different aims and standards, that look for financial support to the same legislature, and the fact that it is thus intrastate means that such organizations as the American Association of Land-Grant Colleges and State Universities, the State Universities Association, and their Joint Office of Institutional Research can be of little assistance in appeasing it.[1]

Many universities today are represented at the state capital by independent bureaucratic lobbies backed by vigorous and highly cohesive alumni groups. The competition among universities often extends to struggles over the right to be the exclusive providers of certain types of programs. The weakness that comes from lack of cohesion has led many governmental bodies to adopt policies based on favoritism rather than on responsible and objective analysis.

Let me now consider some specific examples of the disarray in public higher education in certain large populous states. I start with Illinois. The educational decision-making in this state reflects a fragmented pattern and a lack of over-all direction and planning. Illinois has been characterized by political competition among and even within its state universities; much of the competition has been unhealthy and fruitless. Illinois has had no machinery with the legal authority or the prestige and status necessary to make decisions based on a comprehensive evaluation of the state's educational problems and needs. The Illinois Office of Education, as explained in the last chapter, has had

---

[1] Gordon N. Ray, "Conflict and Cooperation in Higher Education" in Dexter M. Keezer (ed.), *Financing Higher Education 1960–70*, New York: McGraw-Hill Book Co., Inc., 1959, p. 110.

a highly political past which renders it virtually useless as an instrument of planning. The Illinois School Problems Commission, the state's key agency in public school matters, does not concern itself with any issue involving the state's universities and colleges. The state's universities and colleges have channeled their own grooves of influence into the state legislature. Each has its designated "representatives" in Springfield to espouse its cause. To say that the efforts of these institutions are not coordinated is a gross understatement.

The line dividing the University of Illinois and Southern Illinois University, for example, is not an academic one. Rather, it is political. For more than a decade the two have fought, sometimes quite bitterly, over definitions of role and function. Southern Illinois University, having shaken off its former normal school status, became after World War II the state's most rapidly growing (proportionately) and politically aggressive university. In recent years its president has bundled up all of the educational appeals—the nation's need for teachers and engineers, the lack of opportunity for youngsters in southern regions of the state, the shortage of qualified Ph.D.s—for presentation to the governor and state legislature. He has urged the state to provide funds for buildings and staff—and got them, probably at the expense of other state institutions. Over the bitter opposition of the University of Illinois, he successfully obtained, after several legislative refusals, a school of engineering. The university's most recent venture—and it, too, is highly controversial—is the creation and development of a separate campus at Edwardsville, Illinois, close to the St. Louis metropolitan area.

The success of Southern Illinois University in its competitive struggle with other state institutions, particularly the University of Illinois, does not, of course, rest solely or even primarily on the persuasive powers of its president. The center of this university's political strength lies in a bloc of downstate legislators who, primarily for political reasons, are willing to support most proposals. The extent to which their political careers are contingent upon a university base of support can be seen from one behind-the-scenes occurrence a few years ago. The governor, desperately in need of additional votes in the senate to push his tax program through, called representatives from the areas whose commitment to his program was questionable. In urging them to vote in favor of his tax bill, the governor pointed out that if the measure failed he would be forced to take a dim view of future university budget requests. Needless to say he got the necessary votes.

The University of Illinois, however, is also not without political resources. In a study of Chicago's bid to establish a permanent branch of the University of Illinois in the city, Prof. Edward C. Banfield stated:

> The University, together with allied local interests of Champaign and Urbana, was a powerful force in the legislature. Three of the most powerful legislators came from its district. These—all Republicans—were: Senator Everett R. Peters, Chairman of the Illinois Budgetary Commission and Chairman of the Senate Committee on Committees; Representative Ora D. Dillavou, Chairman of the House Appropriations Committee and, therefore, a member of the Budgetary Commission; and Representative Charles Clabaugh, Chairman of the Illinois School Problem Commission. All three depended in some ways on the University and were often its spokesmen.[1]

Although a university may be able to develop direct and independent lines of access into the legislature, it must sacrifice some of its autonomy to do so. Professor Banfield also reported:

> But the University was also dependent upon them. Senator Peters, the most powerful of the three, was said to regard

[1] Edward C. Banfield, *Political Influence*, New York: The Free Press of Glencoe, 1961, pp. 162–63.

President Henry as a "carpetbagger." "Who the hell is he to tell me how to run a university," he once said to a fellow senator. His remark may have been made in a moment of pique and perhaps should not be taken seriously. One close and reliable observer, at any rate, was of the opinion that Peters generally accepted the policy line of the University. There was no doubt, however, that he could exercise a great deal of influence upon the administration of the University, if he chose to do so.[1]

In such a process of mutual interdependence, no university in its conflicts with other segments of the education system can afford not to expand its base of support. Thus in order to block a move enthusiastically supported by Chicago legislators, to create a branch campus in that city, the university "was not unmindful of other legislators." Banfield reports:

> It [the university] gave each of them [state legislators] four season passes to football games, and every two years it wined and dined them lavishly on a two-day "tour" of the University in May, the season when important bills were coming out of the committees. According to a Chicago legislator, the University used these occasions to extol its Urbana-Champaign campus and to lobby against the Chicago branch—"brainwashing," this ingrate called his entertainment. Under the title of Assistant to the President, the University kept a lobbyist whom Peters amiably called his "errand boy." [2]

Since virtually every state is replete with such activities, I hope I won't be accused of singling out Illinois when I say that such a decision-making process is intolerable given the magnitude of our educational problems.

I am happy to report that Illinois has recently created administrative machinery to bring about more order in the decision-making process, but it has not moved as yet toward the development of a master plan.

[1] *Ibid.*, p. 163.
[2] *Ibid.*, p. 163.

Texas is another state worth looking into. The Commission of Higher Education is this state's answer to the demands for planning. Composed of fifteen members appointed by the governor with senate approval, it serves as a budget coordinating agency rather than a line administrative and/or operating agency. Its primary function is to see that no requests for funds for any of the public-supported colleges and universities go to the legislature without first going through it. The commission defines the role of each institution and approves requests for new programs or enrollment expansion. The legislature also intends no new colleges would be set up in the state (except junior colleges) without prior commission approval.

Reactions to the commission's role are mixed. There are those who regard it as a "joke." A prominently placed education official stated: "Governor Shivers did not appoint many strong people when the Commission was set up and as a result the Commission has not been very effective. The Board of Regents of the University of Texas is much stronger and is a prestige-type board." Conversely, others argue that the commission has "drained off much of the competition among institutions and kept the legislature from playing off one educational lobby against another." But all agree that it has yet to receive the full backing of the state's higher education complex.

The legislature does tend to follow the commission's formula on the allocation of funds to the various institutions. Moreover, the commission seems to have some control over programs and enrollments. But its so-called "birth control" function is another matter. On three separate occasions the state legislature, apparently in response to local pressures, has authorized the creation of new colleges without seeking the commission's approval. Most of the difficulty lies in the commission's lack of control of the junior colleges. Members of the legislature told me that virtually every member was under pressure to allow junior colleges to become four-year institutions. These pressures, they said, were very difficult to resist. "To argue for restrictions on over-all expenditures for education in a conservative state like Texas is a relatively easy thing to do," one legislator told a member of my staff, "but to ignore pressures for the creation or expansion of educational facilities in your home constituency is another matter. You've got to understand," he went on, "that every institution is out for itself, and when this happens education becomes a pork barrel."

Fear of the impact of an uncontrolled junior college movement is by no means confined to Texas. In Georgia, where all publicly supported colleges and universities are under one central board, Chancellor Harmon W. Caldwell stated that he fears junior colleges are going to break out all over the place and, if allowed to grow and expand unchecked, will siphon off state funds and threaten the state universities' programs. "What worries me," he said, "is the apparent promises of members of the legislature to people in their home areas that there will be junior colleges developed in every district." If such colleges do develop, the chancellor thinks they should be under the Board of Regents. "Only in this way will it be possible to plan for higher education in Georgia," he concluded.

The junior college movement has aroused fears of pork-barrel politics in Florida also. In a recent gubernatorial campaign, residents of Pensacola were promised by several candidates for public office that if elected they would convert their junior college into a senior college. Although the promise was not immediately kept, this and similar occurrences prompted the State Superintendent of Public Instruction to request the legislature to appropriate the necessary funds to the Board of Control for the purpose of developing a master plan for public education beyond the public schools, which it did. "If we don't get a master plan soon," he said, "every stop-gap college will want a Ph.D. program and education will become the biggest pork barrel

the state has ever seen." A member of the superintendent's
staff framed the problem a bit differently. He said:

> The legislature has reached a stage where education has be-
> come too big an item for it to confine itself merely to ap-
> propriations. Educators are barraging them with all sorts of
> demands. To protect himself at home, a legislator has to sup-
> port his local institution or proposals for new ones. This brings
> a good deal of logrolling. But many of the same members feel
> that they must hold the line on state expenditures. Unless the
> educators get together no one will know what to predict.

Stories such as these could be heard in state after state.
The politics of education in some states is rapidly becoming
the politics of frustration. In the long run decisions based
on local or personal influence distribution will lower the
quality of an educational program. Furthermore, in the
absence of any state planning, how can anyone seriously
contemplate a nationwide policy?

To be sure, forces are at work in some of the states I
have mentioned to bring about greater coordination and
planning. Many educators, legislators, and budget lay
officials have long recognized that in order to meet the
problems of growth, finance, and diversity in functions and
services some coordination and continuous appraisal of the
education system are both desirable and necessary. But the
full acceptance of such ideas is still alien to many university
administrators and legislators. Indeed, for many of the
reformers, the desire for planning is merely a reflection of
certain naive biases. They, not unlike the metropolitan-area
reformers, have a taste for "symmetry, simplicity and, in
a special sense, logic." Others feel that planning will promote greater efficiency and thereby substantially *reduce*
governmental cost. But frankly these arguments are seldom
persuasive. The convincing argument for planning in
education does not rest merely on logical and abstract
reasoning. Rather, it is based primarily on experience. The
fact is that unless educators can decide on the basic

objectives of the higher education system, and unless they decide which institutions are best equipped to offer specialized programs of instruction and research, completely extraneous considerations will determine the allocation of funds. In other words, state legislatures are increasingly forced to rely on pork-barrel methods in order to make the allocations. In brief, given the fact that resources are limited within any state, legislators must develop some type of system upon which to base their decisions.

Education like other public enterprises must compete for what is available. Educators can face this competition in a number of ways. They can create a framework which minimizes the possibility of vigorous or hostile education lobbies operating in the *public arena*. Another alternative is the establishment of some kind of agency, voluntary or legal, to coordinate publicly supported colleges and universities. A number of states—Wisconsin and Ohio, for example—have done this. Under most of these existing arrangements, long-range plans have not been formulated, although perhaps excessive competition and mutual animosities have been somewhat reduced. The final alternative, and the one most widely followed, is to have decisions made within a context where each institution charts its own political course.

Selection of the latter alternative forces *every segment* of education into the ticklish and complicated business of year-by-year political negotiations. Educational leaders of their respective institutions if progress (apparent or real) is to be maintained must exercise the utmost effort to secure greater resources. In such a system the status, prestige, and frequently the tenure of a university or college president rest almost exclusively on what he is able to wangle out of the state legislature *for his institution*. The attitude of his faculty, alumni, and even student body becomes one which can be conveniently summarized by the now hackneyed political query, "What have you done for me lately?" Sustained effort to "improve" his own institution means that he must be prepared for political action, which includes mobilizing the alumni, establishing political slush funds, entertaining, appointing full-time lobbyists, and stockpiling political favors that can be cashed in at the appropriate time. Not all political behavior of educational leaders can be thus characterized, of course; nevertheless, with a high degree of regularity this is what one finds. When a state has no plan, no clear-cut idea in what direction its educational system should move, public officials are not *compelled* to take into account any criterion other than the power of each educational interest and to decide for themselves which *programs* are politically valuable and which are not.

One hardly needs to argue that state legislatures have no business making political footballs out of substantive educational issues. Yet if the professionals in the field are to have a decisive voice in establishing the broad guidelines of educational policy, then ways must be found to cope with the divisive forces operating American higher education *before* they submit their fate to the ultimate control exercised by those who provide and regulate support.

The Politics of Educational Change: The Case of Pennsylvania

Educational systems were not created in a day, nor will they be changed in short order. Existing patterns of instruction, organization, and financial support reflect the heritage of each state as well as the current pressures and demands. Yet educational systems are adaptable; they are capable of meeting new circumstances. This does not happen by accident, but rather through the ingenuity of imaginative leaders. The path to a rational system is far from smooth.

To indicate what those who desire to reconstruct an educational system will encounter, let me explore the current situation in one state. I shall thus be able to give the reader a glimpse of the political dimensions and complexities involved in educational planning. I shall also be able to focus attention on the fact that each state has its own special problems. I have selected Pennsylvania as an example primarily because it is a state in transition, where concern about the workings of the educational system has come close to boiling over. Of course, I must caution the reader that any description of this situation in Pennsylvania may even be out of date.

Until recently many close observers of Pennsylvania's higher educational system saw nothing but chaos and confusion. "We are making decisions off the top of our heads," a high-ranking state educational official said. Another reported, "We have no educational system in Pennsylvania; our policy is everyone for himself. We have made some efforts toward more planning, but the traditions and customs of this state place some formidable obstacles in the path of those of us who want to create a more integrated system."

Certainly Pennsylvania's total educational system has its share of stormy weather. Contrasting Pennsylvania with California, for example, seems to confirm the statement made above that the former state "has no educational system." For years, Pennsylvania has had no statewide higher educational leadership worthy of the name. There was no plan, and disorganization often appeared to handicap the machinery that did exist. In the final report of the Governor's Committee on Education presented in 1961 it was stated:

> There is no one over-all policy-making and central administrative group. Administrative functions are fragmented throughout state government. Fiscal control powers which are at the heart of proper administration do not exist. Nothing remotely

resembling a master plan for higher education exists. Nor does any arrangement exist for bringing such a plan into existence.[1]

The disorganization of the state's higher educational system is clearly illustrated by the way public-private endeavors are combined for state support. Of the approximately 130 institutions offering various types of higher education, only fourteen are four-year state colleges. These institutions, with a combined enrollment of some 27,984 students (approximately 10 per cent of the state's total) have until most recently been engaged exclusively in teacher training. In 1962 ten of the state colleges initiated programs other than teacher education, but in general, students in these programs constitute a very small portion of the total enrollment (less than 5 per cent).

The administration of the fourteen state colleges was conducted by the state superintendent of public instruction, but allowed many of the essential ingredients of institutional autonomy to be preserved. Each institution has its own board of trustees, consisting of nine members appointed by the governor and the superintendent for overlapping six-year terms. Budget and program-change recommendations were channeled first through each board of trustees and next through a fourteen-member board composed of the state college presidents. Ultimate public authority over the state colleges rests, however, in the state legislature and the governor, both of whom must approve all budget requests. Until recently, the State Council of Education, a predominantly professional educational board, coordinated all of the state colleges' activities; its approval was required for all program changes. In compliance with the constitutional mandates, the legislature had early designated the State Department of Public Instruction and the State Council of Education as the two state agencies that were to be concerned with the problems of higher education.

[1] Committee on Education, *The Final Report*, April 1961, p. 20.

Although secure in their control of the state colleges, the roots of these agencies' power were never deep in terms of higher education in general. In a preliminary report on a master plan for higher education, Dr. Charles Boehm, the gubernatorially appointed state superintendent wrote: "The traditional practice of private institutions seeking state fiscal support through direct access to the legislature and budget officials has eliminated the State Council of Education from effective direction in higher education." In the same report, the superintendent said, "The State is not negligent in its support. However, this support is not well-coordinated. The weakness of the present fiscal support plan is well known. This has resulted in needless competition and duplication." [1]

The so-called state-aided institutions carry the bulk of Pennsylvania's higher educational load. Fifteen institutions fall within this category; unlike the situation in other states, essentially private universities have for years obtained some state funds. Pennsylvania State University can be considered as the public state university, but three other large institutions, the University of Pittsburgh and the University of Pennsylvania and Temple University, are among the fifteen. A powerful tradition of institutional independence and autonomy provides the essential ingredient of state-aided colleges and universities. There has been little or no control of the programs of these private colleges and universities by state educational authorities. Support has come from the state legislature on a "negotiated basis"; that is, each senator becomes the bargaining agent of the institution in his district. That is, the state-aided institutions' bargaining power for state resources does not rest simply on riding the popular wave in favor of more education. Rather such power comes basically from a process "which allows

[1] Charles H. Boehm, *Preliminary Proposals for the Development of Guidelines for a Master Plan for Higher Education in Pennsylvania*, March, 1962.

local legislators and political officials to build a record in support of education."

Pennsylvania State University, whose source of educational strength lies in its programs of agriculture and engineering, received a total appropriation for operating costs in 1963–1964 of approximately $25 million. This amount was approximately $8 million more than was appropriated for all fourteen state colleges. The legislature has been left to decide which institutions are worthy of support. Thus the decision to allow the state colleges to become multipurpose institutions is indeed confusing. "The decision to make these institutions multipurpose was ridiculous," one educational leader told a member of my staff. "No money was appropriated and no money can be appropriated if the present support scheme remains in force."

One state official put it this way, "Under such a system, the legislature's task becomes simply to assess political influence; there are no professional judgments to rely upon or widely agreed-upon and well-recognized general policies to follow." Part of the difficulty has resulted from the fact that the agencies concerned with the total state policy were politically weak. The State Department of Public Instruction and the State Council of Education would have had to have prestige and status to bring order out of the chaos of conflicting demands from twenty-nine institutions. If they had the reputation enjoyed by the New York Board of Regents, they might have exercised an influence over the state's universities and colleges. But neither of the two had such a reputation. The council has been vigorously attacked as a "rubber stamp" of the Department of Public Instruction and as a "tool" of the professors of pedagogy. The department has not been immune from attack either. It has been charged that it has little strength and a narrow perspective. Though the department's influence over the state colleges has been extensive, whatever strength it possessed elsewhere in the area of higher education has been dissipated on insignificant issues without ever facing the state's main educational problems.

The department, which undoubtedly is a cut above the usual run of state educational agencies, has had over the years an extremely close political relationship with the P S E A (Pennsylvania State Education Association, the state affiliate of N E A), which is composed primarily of public school teachers and administrators. These two agencies, one public and one private, are the main components of the educational establishment which for many years has had the major hand in the management of the state's public schools and state colleges and in the presentation of their needs to the legislature. But a few years ago the wheel of political fortune took a complete turn, and the power and authority of this establishment were seriously challenged.

The issue that proved to be quite disruptive and which virtually immobilized all efforts of the existing state machinery to formulate plans for higher education emerged in the 1959 session of the Pennsylvania legislature. The issue itself did not directly involve higher education, but, as we shall see, it had important implications for it. The Pennsylvania Education Association, in collaboration with the Association of State School Directors and the Department of Public Instruction, introduced legislation to (a) increase substantially the salaries of teachers; and (b) provide more money for this purpose by increasing state aid, which was already geared to support approximately 50 per cent of all public school operating costs. For at least two years previous to this the state legislature had steadfastly refused to appropriate additional state funds for this purpose. But these new demands were introduced at a time when the public was up in arms over the quality of the educational system, a protest generated largely by the launching of the first Soviet sputnik. Undoubtedly the intense public concern over education entered into the calculations of those requesting greater support for public schools. In brief, the political climate seemed especially propitious for them to make vigorous and unrelenting demands for increased state aid.

Although fully cognizant of the public concern over improving the quality of public education, the Pennsylvania state legislature and the governor were generally adhering to a conservative policy; they were willing only to yield a little bit here and there. The state had at one time an accumulated deficit of approximately $140 million. But the forces demanding change appeared to have a wide base of support. The demands also came at a time when the governor and legislature were keenly conscious of the fact that those who demanded *no increase* in taxation seemed to have a powerful following. In any event, it appears to have been the opinion of the majority of the state legislators and the governor that the new demands were out of proportion to the possible resources of the state unless one contemplated a drastic increase in taxation. To fight its way out of this dilemma, the legislature exercised a power that is frequently and conveniently invoked by legislative bodies when serious conflict threatens the established order. Late in 1959 the chairman of the House Education Committee, Jeanette F. Reibman, introduced a resolution asking the governor to appoint a committee to consider education at all levels in the state of Pennsylvania. The Pennsylvania Education Association, having been unsuccessful in its attempts to get any money bills passed, endorsed the resolution, as did the Department of Public Instruction. The legislature eventually passed the resolution and the governor appointed the committee, later to be known as the Committee of a Hundred. It is important to note that there were no representatives of the educational establishment on the committee, which was an exclusively lay body. Included in its membership were a United States Senator, the lieutenant-governor, members of the state senate and house of representatives, judges, and prestigious citizens from various professional, business and labor, and civic fields. The committee divided itself into eight task forces dealing with subjects ranging from state finances to teacher certification. The bulk of the committee's work concerned the public schools and teacher education. However, since more than half of the teachers prepared in the states were educated in the fourteen state colleges, clearly school politics and higher education politics were unavoidably scrambled together.

Although interpretations vary with individual viewpoints, what might be called "an anti-professional education bloc" seems to have emerged in the state in 1959. This bloc was perhaps more loosely organized than the establishment it opposed, but was intent on wrenching control of the public schools and the fourteen state colleges from what one observer called the "P E A, the Department of Public Instruction, and their crowd." Indeed, more than one informant stated that the committee really masked a power struggle in which high-ranking state officials, including the governor and leading legislators, were determined to reduce and minimize the influence of the state educational establishment.

There is little doubt that the educational establishment considered the committee a threat to its position. The committee claimed in its final report that a number of members of the educational profession were consulted and that "their professional advice was of great importance." But few in the opposing camp accepted these statements as facts. The committee's executive secretary was portrayed as the governor's hatchet man and was widely accused of engineering a conspiracy against the department and the P E A. Certainly, when the report was finally submitted to the legislature in 1961, the educational establishment found much cause to object, particularly to those sections of the report pertaining to teacher education and certification.

After a rather vigorous political battle, the establishment was able to muster enough votes in the state senate to kill what it considered the objectionable recommendations of the report. But the establishment did not emerge from the struggle with its power intact; indeed the struggle still goes on. The election of a governor of another party has had no discernible effect on the general dimensions of the struggle. What seems to have been generally agreed upon by all those in opposition to the influence wielded by the educational establishment was that some way had to be found to infiltrate the tightly knit network of relationships among professional educators that had developed over the years.

But before I discuss this I should point out that in the political context of Pennsylvania it is small wonder that relatively little progress has been made in the formulation of a master plan for higher education. Other factors, to be sure, contributed to the state's incapacity to devise plans for coordination and control of higher education, but in the final analysis it seems that lack of confidence in the professional education domination of the fourteen state colleges and the Department of Public Instruction as well as heavy budgetary strains were the causes of the failure.

That the Pennsylvania system of higher education invites critics, few can deny. Numerous responsible state officials and citizens have called for a master plan. The governor's committee recommended that a "master plan be developed at the earliest possible moment." What stands in the way? Lack of any machinery that enjoys public confidence has been one factor. Certainly the two state agencies feeling the brunt of a major political onslaught could hardly be expected to expand their operations successfully; these agencies were not able to protect and preserve what authority they possessed. But this is not all. Vested interest in the *status quo* is an equally significant factor. Defenders of the system contend that under existing conditions each institution is permitted to act as a separate entity and develop its own programs free of outside intervention. Central planning, they argue, would undermine each faculty's capacity to decide which programs it is best suited and equipped to offer. They rest their case on the assertion that diversity and independence have made the American educational system as a whole the best in the world.

The pertinence and merit of such arguments are subject to serious question. In reality, genuine reform of Pennsylvania's education system is impeded by the fact that those who have been able to gain political advantage are very reluctant, to say the least, to surrender their vested interests. However, distress with the educational situation in Pennsylvania (part brought on by financial pressures and part brought on by a concern with improving the *quality* of education) has become sufficiently acute for the state legislature to alter basically the state's administrative machinery for governing education at all levels. In 1963, the State Council of Education was abolished.

How the state is to plan for education, what responsibilities the state will assume in the field of higher education —these are the concerns of the newly created State Board of Education. The board is to consist of "seventeen members, seven of whom shall also serve as members of the Council on Basic Education [and] seven of whom shall serve as members of the Council of Higher Education and three of whom shall be members at large." Each member is appointed by the governor (subject to senatorial confirmation) for a six-year term. Under the terms of the statute, not more than two members serving on each council and none of the members at large shall be employed in an educational enterprise. The superintendent of public instruction is designated as the "chief Executive Officer" of the board and is entitled to attend all meetings but has no vote. The powers and duties of the board and the two councils are broadly defined. Of concern here is Section 1319, which states that the Council of Higher Education shall have the power to:

1. Develop a master plan for higher education in the Commonwealth, including a system of community colleges as provided by law.

2. Review the annual budget requests of institutions of higher education.

3. Develop standards for the approval of colleges and universities for the granting of certificates and degrees.

4. Develop standards for all higher education building projects involving the use of State funds or the funds of any Commonwealth instrumentality and

5. Investigate programs, conduct research studies and formulate policy proposals in all areas pertaining to higher education in the Commonwealth, including a system of community colleges and technical institutes as provided by law.

Those who wonder about Pennsylvania's educational future must reserve their judgments until the new board gets into full swing (at the time of this writing the governor has just made his appointments). The political course for any new governmental agency is seldom an easy one. Moreover it takes considerable time for people to learn to reconcile their views concerning what ought to be done with what can in reality be done. It takes time for a governmental agency to gain the public confidence necessary for the effective implementation of its policies. (Unquestionably the new board will find itself subject to political pressures it never dreamed existed.) For example, officials at Temple University have already announced their desire to have Temple become the state's major university—a goal that obviously conflicts with the aspirations of Pennsylvania State University officials. In short, the obstacles to educational planning are still formidable in Pennsylvania, though perhaps less so than before. Despite all these negative thoughts, the prospects for introducing rationality into Pennsylvania's educational system are strong. The new proposed arrangement for planning and coordination represents a significant transition from an arena of unresolved conflict for legislative and gubernatorial decision-making to one requiring a sorting of alternatives before decisions are made. The lessons of power have been learned; at least a number of Pennsylvanians hope so.

The Private Colleges and Universities

In the next chapter I shall report encouraging developments in policy making in education in the two most populous states of the Union, California and New York. Before examining what has been done and is projected in these two highly important states I must examine a complication of policy making that exists in the United States alone. I refer to the very important role played by private colleges and universities, both secular and church-connected. The reader who has any doubt of this should turn back to page 12 and examine Table 2. The role of the private institution in education *beyond the high school* is far greater than the part played by private elementary and secondary schools. Any attempt to try and lump together all private institutions—schools, colleges, and universities—in one category is a great mistake. The arguments in favor of public schools as an instrument of democracy do not apply to colleges and universities. In the first place, compulsory attendance laws have never extended to the college the age of college attendance; in the second place, the colleges are traditionally committed to some form of selection (with the exception of the two-year community college); in the third place, private colleges and universities historically have often been national institutions, drawing their students from all sections of the nation; and lastly, in terms of the percentage of college graduates, the private institutions are nearly as significant as the public.

Looking at the educational scene in the entire United States, we thus see that in addition to the complications introduced by the educational sovereignty of fifty states, we have a split in the higher educational ranks between private and public institutions. The split is far less apparent than it was thirty years ago during the depression years, when both types of institution were competing for students and money. The leaders of both categories now generally agree each needs the other. Yet the attitude of the administrators and professors in private colleges and universities toward the state and the Federal government is bound to be different. In most states the educational authorities have a hands-off policy toward the private institutions, although legally the state could greatly influence the curricula and even close the institution. Only in one state (Pennsylvania) do private institutions turn to the state capital as a major source of funds. Today the eyes of the college presidents are directed to Washington.

When I come to examine New York we shall see how hard it is to shape educational policy in a state with many powerful private institutions. I anticipate what will thereby be made apparent by suggesting that it may be well to distinguish among the following functions performed by colleges and universities.

1. Provision of a general so-called liberal arts program.

2. Education for the professions and semi-professions culminating in a bachelor's or master's degree (except the education of teachers and engineers).

3. Education of teachers for the public schools.

4. Education of engineers.

5. Post-bachelor programs leading to the doctor's degree.

6. Education of lawyers.

7. Education of medical men.

These categories are not completely inclusive, but I could demonstrate that well over 90 per cent of all students fit into them.

Categories 1 and 2 merge and include all those courses of study given by undergraduate schools of business or departments of commerce. All students in the first four classes are characterized by the fact that if they have a vocational orientation, it is well advanced before the first degree is obtained. In contrast, those in the last three have usually obtained a bachelor's degree before entering on their professional studies. But again, the dividing lines are far from sharp. The numbers involved in 1, 2, 3, and 4 are large. The percentage of an age group involved may before long amount to 30 per cent. The numbers in the other classes are very much smaller—far too small for the national welfare—not over 3 per cent of an age group at present. Another difference is important. The faculties or schools within a university providing education for future Ph.D. holders, lawyers, and medical men tend to attract students from many states and send their graduates to many states. In other words, I would consider categories 5, 6, and 7 essentially national whether carried out by state-supported or private institutions. This means that planning the future of professional and graduate schools of private universities as well as state universities should be on a national basis. But, as I shall try to make evident in the last chapter, such a national undertaking must first include planning on a state basis. I shall conclude this chapter by an analysis of the relation of the state to private institutions of higher education. In so doing I hope to lay the basis for my subsequent discussion of planning at the national level, which must include private and public institutions.

It is interesting that in the O E C D document to which I referred in Chapter 1, we find these sentences:

Another basic issue is the conflict between public and private institutions. It is a matter of history that the older elite centers of research were private . . . Certainly the California master plan offers, and Berkeley already demonstrates, the possibility of establishing the highest quality on a massive popular base. There can surely be no case against federal encouragement to state institutions capable of matching the quality of Yale or Princeton, but again we would emphasize *not* at the expense of the private institutions . . .

The authors go on to say that they would urge "even more emphasis on the overriding national character of graduate schools and their problems. Private or public institutions seem to us to converge rather than to differentiate. The broad aim of policy must be to encourage a wide geographical spread of the highest possible quality."

If the reader will turn back to Chapter 1, he will note from Table 2 that private institutions easily outnumber public ones. In terms of enrollment, however, the situation is reversed. Just over 59 per cent of the *total* enrollment was in public institutions, and the figure seems likely to increase in the coming years. The fastest rates of growth in the period 1955–1960 were among the public junior colleges and the slowest were among the private four-year institutions. I have not been able to obtain exact figures as to the distribution of students among private and public universities either at the graduate or undergraduate level. Something like 30 per cent of the entire college and university enrollment is in liberal arts colleges (which are almost without exception private). I venture to estimate that of the total *undergraduate* enrollment about half is in private colleges or universities, and about half in state colleges and state universities. There are 764 liberal arts colleges and about 50 or 60 private institutions which entitle themselves universities. Let me examine the relation of the state to these institutions insofar as these undergraduate nonprofessional programs are concerned (categories 1 and 2 page 71).

I pointed out earlier that in theory an individual state can closely examine a private educational institution and close it if the duly constituted authorities so decided. A few states have for many years taken very seriously their responsibility for general supervision of private educational institutions. New York State is the outstanding example. In my opinion, every state should seek to follow New

York. This does not mean that the state would set any limits to the nature of the liberal arts curriculum. It would do no more than the regional accrediting agencies seek to do, which is to distinguish between clearly fraudulent institutions and all the others. Four years of attendance at the institution, a certain minimum of library and laboratory facilities, a general impression of the size and quality of the staff is about all that can be demanded in the interest of the prospective students and their parents.

The American public long ago endorsed the principle of free competition among institutions private and public insofar as the bachelor's degree is concerned, *except for the professions*. A so-called liberal or general education program leading to a bachelor's degree can include almost anything and there are no recognized standards of admission for students or for the degree itself. As a consequence, as everyone knows, holding a bachelor's degree has no significance. The informed citizen always asks, "From what college did you graduate?" The admission officers of our graduate and professional schools ask the same question, and each has his own list of colleges ranked roughly according to the standards required for graduation. Experience in some law schools has shown that a student with an A record from certain undergraduate colleges has about the same chance of obtaining a law degree as students with a C average from other colleges.

Since the American public long ago decided that a bachelor's degree might mean anything, it would be a losing battle for each of the fifty states to attempt to determine a minimum level of competence for this degree. I am inclined to think the same is true of the master's degree except insofar as this degree is given for professional work as, indeed, the vast majority are.

What the state should do is to close down fraudulent "diploma mills." A pamphlet issued in 1960 by the American Council on Education states that: "American degree mills are identified as certain institutions calling themselves colleges or universities which confer 'quick way' (usually mail order) degrees on payment of a fee. These institutions turn out bachelor's, master's or doctor's degrees without requiring the labor, thought and attention usually expected of those who earn such degrees." The authors conclude that the "estimate of one hundred bogus degree-granting universities and colleges is quite modest. One association that represents many of these phony colleges and universities, and maintains a seal of approval for their use, states that their annual business amounts to $75,000,000 and that their enrollment in one recent year was 750,000 students."

The American Council pamphlet points out the many practical and legal difficulties involved in implementing state legislation aimed at eliminating degree mills, but it also points out that in 1960 only very few states had adequate laws. Thirty-four states have *no* legislation specifically mentioning correspondence schools, and twenty-six states have no legal control over educational institutions granting degrees. What is clearly needed in most states is first legislation, then strengthening of the state authorities charged with enforcement, and lastly some basis for exchange of information among the states. As to the last point, I shall have more to say in the concluding pages of this book.

Assuming that state educational authorities are in a position to close clearly fraudulent institutions, the question is to what further degree should the state attempt to insure the quality of education provided by private colleges and universities? To answer this question, I return to my seven categories and note the difficulty of laying down standards for the degrees. As far as categories 1 and 2 are concerned, I suggest the state make no attempt to enforce standards. (I might add that I think the regional accrediting agencies had better give up trying to do the job as well.) I do believe, however, that publication of standardized information by the state about such institutions might be worthwhile. Laws requiring the submission of such simple facts as numbers of students, faculty, degrees granted in various fields, and criteria for admission could not be taken by honest educators as undue state control.

I now turn to the relation of the state to private institutions, many of whose graduates are in categories 3 to 6 (page 71). Of these, by far the most are preparing to be teachers in our public schools. Since I have written a volume on the education of teachers for our public schools and made specific recommendations as to the relation of the state to the institutions preparing teachers, I shall not discuss the subject further here. Since a large percentage of the teachers prepared in most states find employment within the state, the planning for the expansion of teacher education should be in the first instance on a state-by-state basis. The same may well be true of engineers in many states, and even of lawyers and doctors. What I suggest in all the cases of professional training is first an assessment of the actual situation in each state, a projection of future supply and demand, and then a procedure for bringing together the state estimates on a national basis and the calculation of the migration of professional people trained in one state to another. Such problems together with the question of Federal financial aid to education will be discussed in the concluding chapter of this book.

It is important to note that the issue of private versus public institutions is not the issue of national as compared to state planning. It is true that some dozen or so private universities because of their history stand out as national centers for professional training and research. But if we think of future engineers, doctors, and lawyers (a very small proportion of the entire post-high-school student body), one cannot say that those professionally trained in a state university stay within the state while those prepared in the private institutions are scattered over fifty states. Except for the unique role played by the private four-year liberal arts college, there is no reason to treat the support of private and public institutions separately in terms of shaping policy.

Federal Assistance to Higher Education

It is interesting to note that the legislation passed by Congress in late 1963, to which I have already referred, includes provisions designed to assist private as well as public institutions by Federal grants. These include grants for construction of undergraduate academic facilities (there are certain limitations on the type of structure to be erected with Federal money by private institutions), grants for construction of graduate academic facilities, and loans for construction of academic facilities. Through the National Defense Education Act of 1958 as amended in 1963, provisions are made for loans to students in institutions of higher education by an authorized appropriation of $125 million for the first year and $135 million for the next. As in the original bill, the benefits of this legislation are open to students in both private and public colleges and universities. The same bill includes sections to strengthen science, mathematics, and modern foreign language instruction and provides for national defense fellowships, all of which can be considered as Federal assistance to higher education in general, irrespective of whether it is private or public.

The findings and declarations of policy in the newly amended National Defense Education Act may serve to epitomize the concern of the Congress of the United States with education, which so far has been chiefly manifest through Federal aid to higher education. Section 101 reads as follows:

> The Congress hereby finds and declares that the security of the Nation requires the fullest development of the mental resources and technical skills of its young men and women. The present emergency demands that additional and more

adequate educational opportunities be made available. The defense of this Nation depends upon the mastery of modern techniques developed from complex scientific principles. It depends as well upon the discovery and development of new principles, new techniques, and new knowledge.

We must increase our efforts to identify and educate more of the talent of our Nation. This requires programs that will give assurance that no student of ability will be denied an opportunity for higher education because of financial need; will correct as rapidly as possible the existing imbalances in our educational programs which have led to an insufficient proportion of our population educated in science, mathematics, and modern foreign languages and trained in technology.

In examining the national scene, one finds that demands for expanding educational opportunities in higher education are colliding head-on with demands for a more efficient and rational distribution of resources to keep tax levels at reasonable minimums. Despite all the study and talk, I feel there is still too strong a tendency to underestimate the magnitude of the demands facing our system of higher education—demands that cry out the need for greater planning. For example, in 1963 about 4½ million students were enrolled in higher education. The projected enrollments for 1975 place this figure at over 8½ million. The estimated expenditures required for expansion of physical facilities needed for higher education in 1963 is $1,692,000,-000. By 1975, that figure is expected to reach $32,946,000,-000. Such changes will obviously require additional sources of revenue, with the most likely source being tax dollars. The costs in dollars for students (and parents) have been rising sharply since 1956, as shown in Table 5. The O E C D examiners, pointing to these figures, state that "of the total increase in college costs between 1928 and 1960, approximately one third took place in the last four years. On the other hand, average family incomes rose 14 per cent in these years and enrollment is increasing fastest in the less costly public institutions." The increase in loan funds certainly has assisted students to attend the more expensive institutions and a Federal scholarship policy might do even more. My own view tends to be in favor of loans for undergraduate nonprofessional education and state scholarships for future teachers as well as Federal scholarships for medical students and those working for the Ph.D.

As these problems come rapidly upon us, only a few states have responded with a fresh approach to solve them, and except for certain interstate compacts no mechanism exists for interstate cooperation. The seriousness of the situation is equaled only by the inadequacy of the political response to meet it.

Table 5. Costs of College Education, 1928–1960
(U. S. Dollars Per Annum)

Type of Institution	Total Costs (Tuition Fees, Room & Board)				
	1928	1940	1952	1956	1960
Large Public (State Resident Students)	405	461	731	819	988
Small Public (State Resident Students)	366	406	655	722	846
Large Public (Nonresident Students) . .	454	565	950	1076	1316
Small Public (Nonresident Students) . .	403	478	791	908	1143
Large Private......................	733	739	1220	1439	1855
Medium Private....................	536	629	1080	1275	1639

President Johnson in signing the Higher Education Facilities Act of 1963 pointed out that the legislation, which he characterized as "dramatic," was concrete evidence of a renewed and continued national commitment to education as the key to our nation's social and technological and economic and moral progress. Federal assistance will continue to be forthcoming for a loan program, for the building of classrooms for several hundred thousand college students; the erection of many new public community colleges will be assisted, the vocational education program will be modernized and expanded. As the President said,

"Working together, the Congress and the executive branch have made possible the enactment of a series of legislative landmarks in the field of education." All who are worried about our educational future must applaud all those who were concerned with the framing and passage of these Congressional measures.

As one turns the pages of the government document entitled *Selected Education Acts, 1963*, one is struck by the number of times grants to the individual states and through state agencies are mentioned. In one of the acts, the Congress declared, "The States and local communities have and must retain control over and primary responsibility for public education." It is no easy matter to reconcile this basic principle of our Federal structure with the necessity for the expenditure of large amounts of Federal funds at all educational levels. The larger the Federal grants for such specific purposes as named in the 1963 legislation, the greater the need for the shaping of a nationwide educational policy. But I postpone a further discussion of this topic until, in the next chapter, I examine what has happened at the state level in our two largest states.

CHAPTER 4
New York and California

The two most populous states in the Union warrant a close examination by anyone interested in educational policy. They present both similarities and contrast, which make a comparison between them most rewarding. In terms of geography, climate, history, and forecasts of future population, the two areas stand in sharp contrast. In terms of the organization of public education, the contrast, while not as striking, is nevertheless sufficient to make a foreign student of our educational chaos wonder which state is to be taken as typical. The answer, of course, is neither. From the viewpoint of one American observer, namely the author of this volume, each state may be considered as furnishing something *approaching* an ideal solution to *part* of a total problem. California has led the way in providing a rational approach to educational policy making beyond the high school. And for generations, New York has provided a model of how to organize and employ the power of the state to promote excellence in the locally controlled public schools. Leaving New York City aside for the moment, I would be prepared to go so far as to say that if one could imagine combining California's master plan for higher education with New York's Board of Regents and its Commissioner of Education, one would have an example of American public education at its best. Some of the factors hindering such an ideal solution in any state will become apparent as my description of New York and California proceeds. Nevertheless, almost every state in the Union can learn from examining the history and current practices of the educational authorities (including the state universities and colleges) in these two states.

The legislature is the source of authority under every state constitution. But tradition and custom play an enormous role in determining how this authority is employed. And here New York and California are at almost the extreme opposite ends of a wide spectrum of possibilities. The citizens of New York have come to expect that educational policies will not become footballs in the legislative halls, while Californians tend to believe that democracy requires that the legislators resolve all major educational issues. The same difference in spirit is apparent when we realize that, for generations, New York's powerful Board of Regents has been elected by the legislature, and the board in turn appoints the Commissioner of Education (the chief state school officer). Only very indirectly does the voter participate in the establishment of the educational authority. In California on the other hand, the chief school officer is elected. And no one was surprised that in 1962 the voters of the state were asked to decide between two candidates for the post who argued their differences vigorously in a statewide election campaign. In New York State, such an attempt to place educational issues directly before the electorate would be almost unthinkable.

Before proceeding with the comparison of New York and California, I must consider the largest school district (in terms of population) in the nation, namely New York City. The very existence of this school district, with a population of over 7 million yet treated like all other districts by action of the state, is almost a denial of the classic arguments in favor of the American system. Read the explanation of our typical state organization, with its many local boards of education largely independent and responsive to local needs. Then consider New York City as a single school district, which it is, on the same organizational level as a district with a few thousand inhabitants; and then try to explain to a European how we manage our public schools! The position of Superintendent of Schools in New York City is far more nearly comparable to a national minister of education in a small European nation or in one of the German states than to the usual American school super-intendency.

To be sure, the legal responsibility of the New York State educational officials for what goes on in New York City is quite clear. But I think it fair to say that traditionally Albany has let New York City develop its own school system and, in recent years, wrestle with its almost insoluble problems as best it could. When one talks to public school people in Albany, there often creeps into the conversation an unconscious assumption that when one speaks about New York State one is excluding New York City.

The fact that, for a generation at least, state legislators from New York City have been predominantly Democrats while the majority of the legislature has been Republican is not to be ignored. Particularly in connection with the financial support of the public schools, the possibility of a close interplay between partisan politics and school policy is never far distant. I do not propose to discuss the problems of the New York City schools, for to do so would take me away from the central theme of this book, which is shaping educational policy. But two or three facts should be recorded. First the teachers in the New York City schools have never been closely tied to a comprehensive organization affiliated with either the N E A or the New York State Teachers Association. Within the last decade a chapter of the American Federation of Teachers (often referred to as the teacher's union) has been successful in negotiating a contract with the Board of Education.

Long before this operation, however, the public school people in New York City could not be considered an active component of the New York State establishment. There are many reflections of this situation. One is the fact that the comprehensive high school has never been as wholeheartedly welcomed in New York City as elsewhere. The existence of a number of selective academic high schools, as well as many vocational high schools, makes the New York City school system an exception to what one can write in general about secondary education in the United States. One might say one of the dogmas of the N E A has never been accepted in New York City, namely that all public school pupils should attend a comprehensive high school. A second dogma which has never been accepted in principle is that all teachers, kindergarten through grade 12, should be on equal footing and paid according to the same salary schedule. Before the teacher's union became powerful, attempts of the N E A to recruit members from New York City schools failed, in part because the high school teachers (who had a separate organization) repudiated the idea of a uniform salary schedule. To one accustomed to looking at the European scene, with its highly selective secondary schools with a separate group of teachers, New York City seems almost European. For the ambitious, intellectually able students, such a system has advantages. No one can deny this. As to the disadvantages of such a system, one might say it is not as able to cope with the unambitious, intellectually incapable boy or girl as the typical American school district.

Leaving aside the pros and cons of the New York City system as compared with that of, let us say, Los Angeles or San Francisco, the interesting question is: Who determined the policy of New York City? I venture the hypothesis that the attempt of the public school people in the 1920s to put the *Cardinal Principles* into effect in New York City failed because the European tradition in the high schools was so powerful. Furthermore, employers and labor union officials favored a part-time education for the youth headed for the vocation of skilled labor. When the depression hit, these part-time schools for one type of youth were converted to full time vocational schools, which exist in New York City as nowhere else in the United States.

After World War II, if you asked who shaped policy in the New York City schools, the usual answer was, the politicians. The reference was to the intermeshing of the wheels within wheels of the public school teachers and administrators on the one hand and the practical politician on the other. In the late 1950s the voices of the critics of a political school system became louder. Signs of growing inefficiency, if not corruption, in the building and maintenance of schools were clearly visible. Taking advantage of a cleavage within the Democratic Party, a small group of reformers were able to persuade the state legislature, in special session, to change the law which regulated the appointment of school board members. The then-existing board was practically discharged by legislative fiat in a very unusual action in which there was almost no dissent in either the Democratic or Republican party. This is an illustration of the fact that the legislature in any state may step directly into the educational system and make its will felt if both parties are in favor of an action and public opinion demands it.

Following a practice developed in Chicago some years before, the new law provided for the establishment of a panel of prominent citizens from which the mayor had to choose in appointing the board members. (The old method, it was charged, had resulted in essentially political appointments.) The procedure was followed and an excellent board took office and proceeded to choose an outstanding man as superintendent. Clearly policy for the New York schools is entering a new phase. It is unlikely that the establishment, as I have been using the word, will have much influence, since it has not been effective in the past and since the strongly anti-N E A United Federation of Teachers is in a position to deal directly with the school board. It is unlikely that Albany will play a predominant role. It will be interesting to see how decisions will be made and what decisions will be under these new conditions. Of one thing we may be sure: policy making will not be easy in face of the explosive problems presented by the terrible conditions in the Negro slums and the intemperate demands of many Negro leaders for the *immediate* introduction of mixed schools at all levels and in all sections of the city; it may be necessary for the state to play a more active role, as I suggested in Chapter 2.

With this large parenthesis about New York City, I now turn to a comparison of policy making in New York State (exclusive of New York City) and in California. The general pattern of the public schools is much the same. The public school people have over the years implemented the "cardinal principles": the comprehensive high school is accepted as the American type of public secondary school. However, as I indicated earlier, the public school people in New York, though in amicable relations with the state officials, play a secondary role as compared to what has been the case in California. The continued existence of the Regents Examinations, to which I have already referred, is evidence of the contrast I have in mind. The leadership shown by the New York commissioner in facing the educational revolution, to which I also referred earlier, is another example. But the revision of the certification requirements in New York and California provide an insight into the difference in the two states. Surely the state requirements for teacher certification and *particularly the way they are changed* present a picture of policy making in a given state.

The New York story is quickly and simply told. The legislature long ago delegated to the Board of Regents and the Commissioner of Education the power to regulate how teachers were to be educated—that is, of course, teachers who were to be employed in New York. This delegation of authority underlines the essential elements in New York State which I have already emphasized. Using this delegated authority, the Board of Regents has altered from time to time the certification rules and procedures. When, in 1957, at the time of the Russian success with sputnik, a wave of bitter criticism of public schools and public school teachers swept the nation, the citizens of New York reacted in characteristic fashion. The critics of the existing certification rules, though distrusting the public school people, never thought of taking their case to the legislature. Instead they turned their attention to the Board of Regents and the commissioner's office. The state officials were already alerted to the changing public mood. In two separate undertakings, the state educational machinery went into action to explore the interests of different groups who were concerned with the education of elementary and secondary school teachers. In each case, great care was taken to hear a variety of different views. Through committees and subcommittees and a request for written opinions, the opinions of all interested parties were examined. The final documents were sets of regulations of the state educational authorities, not laws passed by the legislature. The point is all-important. Whether or not one agrees with the final outcome, it is certain that policy was not determined by any one group. The public school people did not control the situation ultimately by ignoring the state authorities, as in Indiana, or by controlling the state machinery, as in New Jersey. Policy was determined by state officials on the basis of a careful exploration of opinion of *all* groups of educators and the general public. To my mind, this is how state educational policy should be evolved.

The contrast with California is striking, but to bring it out I must relate a rather long and complicated story.

The impact of sputnik on California was as great as in any part of the Union. The nationwide attack on public schools and on professors of education was welcomed by leading professors of the liberal arts in the University of California and in private educational institutions. Indeed, for more than a decade the hostility between the professors of education and the rest of the faculty at Berkeley had been notorious. It must be recorded as a fact that an influential body of citizens had come to believe, rightly or wrongly, that the California secondary and elementary schools were not as good as they should be. Elementary education was called too "soft," and accused of using the "wrong method" of teaching reading; secondary education was under attack for inadequate preparation of those entering the university which, however, selected only about the top 15 per cent. The failure of many entering freshmen to write clearly was one point of criticism.

In 1959, I was asked to speak in California to a subcommittee of a Citizens Advisory Commission that had been appointed by the legislature. Some members of this committee were breathing fire and hostility to professors of education and all their works. Indeed, at a cocktail party in Palo Alto, I was told by a prominent citizen long active in local public school affairs that he saw no hope for the schools in California until there was a radical reform of schools of education!

The commission heard a vast number of witnesses. It made no less than 104 recommendations. Three touched on the certification issue and the education of teachers, and can be considered as curtain-raisers to the legislative battle which was to come. For example, one of the recommendations was, "The Commission recommends to the new governing board for the state colleges that a reduction in the number of courses in education offered in the state colleges be instituted."

Two other recommendations were addressed to the *legislature* (this is an important point), asking the legislature to standardize elementary and secondary certificates. (There was only one dissent.) A novel feature of one of the recommendations was that a subject matter major other than education "and a year of postgraduate study" be required for future elementary teachers. The secondary credential was to be based on five years (as was then the practice) and "a subject matter major appropriate for secondary school teaching, other than education, and an area of specialization or a subject minor; and a teaching major of at least 36 semester hours and a teaching minor of at least 20 semester hours."

Long before this Citizens Advisory Commission rendered its report a body of educators had started work on revising the requirements for credentials. As early as 1954 the California Council on Teacher Education (composed largely of educators and including one representative of the California Teachers Association) recommended a drastic overhaul of certification requirements. On December 7, 1954, to be exact, the president of the council and the superintendent of public instruction jointly appointed a fourteen-member state committee to make the required study. The pace of their work was leisurely and the report was rendered only in May 1957. In November of the same year, the committee's report was accepted by the council and widely circulated. Seven public meetings were held to discuss the recommendations, and after an analysis of the testimony, the State Department of Education in 1958–1959 held eight public meetings. Finally, a proposed new credential structure was presented by the department to the council in October 1959 and accepted. More discussions with various groups followed and the superintendent presented the recommendations to the *state Board of Education* in January 1960 at a public hearing. In February 1960 the board approved the new credential structure, which was based upon fourteen general principles that the board believed should underlie a structure designed for the certification of professional staff members of the public schools.

It was at this meeting that an apparently harmless word was introduced that was to be the storm center of the legislative battle a year later. The word was "academic," and it seems quite clear that the state board (not dominated by the public school people), in accepting the report of the council, introduced the distinction between academic and non-academic majors for future teachers in response to the vigorous critics of the public schools.

At this point the differences between New York and California become increasingly apparent. From 1954 to 1960 state officials, working harmoniously with the public school people, were revising the rules which were to govern the education of teachers. Unlike New York, California appears to have made no effort to hear from the liberal arts professors in the state, some of whom had long been hard critics of the schools and the preparation of teachers. By the time the leisurely report of the council reached the state Board of Education, the composition of the board had been changed by new appointments by the governor. The board seems to have been of two minds as to how far to go to meet the demands of the critics of public school people. After introducing the word "academic" in February 1960, in December of the same year the board broadened the definition to include "such courses in the arts as deal with criticism, theory and history"; then a month later they eliminated the definition from the legislation that was to be recommended to the legislature. This was the signal for battle. Senator Fisher of San Diego proceeded to introduce a bill into the legislature that became known as the Fisher Bill. In it, the forces that had been so long hostile to the educational establishment thought they had found a banner around which to rally. The pros and cons of the Fisher Bill and its amendments were argued around the state and in legislative committee meetings for the next six months. Whether in fact the battle was largely a sham battle, as I am inclined to think, the fact that the issue was fought out in the legislature is what differentiates educational policy making in California from that in New York. And the history of the Fisher Bill shows how easy it is for educational issues to become entangled with partisan issues when reformers take their case to a state legislature.

In following the details of the legislative struggle over the Fisher Bill, the reader must remember first that a climate of opinion hostile to public schools and professors of education had been growing in intensity since sputnik in 1957, and second, that in the fall of 1962, an election for governor was to take place in which Governor Pat Brown might be faced by Richard M. Nixon, a formidable opponent, or so it was then thought. Certainly the credential legislation finally passed was not a purely Democratic affair, but it seems evident that the leaders of the Democratic Party were far from loath to take advantage of the hostility to professors of education already manifested in several recommendations in the final report of the Citizens Advisory Commission late in 1960.

As to the influence of the election of 1962, it is not without significance that on April 28, 1961, the governor said:

> I want to declare my unqualified support [of the Fisher Bill], and I intend to do everything proper to urge the members of the Assembly Education Committee to approve it in its present form. I think that you will recall in my address to

the Legislature I stated that I wanted just such a bill—I think there have been some very substantial amendments but the purpose of the bill—to see that the teachers major in solids in contrast to working on how to teach courses—is basic in the bill and it's still there.

In answer to a question as to whether the California Teachers Association had opposed the bill the governor said, "Yes, they have. They made a personal call upon this office and told me that by action of their Legislative Committee they were opposed to it. They agreed in principle with the bill but they didn't want the bill signed; they wanted it sent over to an interim committee."

Later in the testimony Governor Brown said, "Right after I was elected Governor I met with the C T A officials and I had their support in the legislative program affecting education in my first session and I have enjoyed a very fine relationship with them and I respect their views, but I just think that they're wrong in this case."

Still another extract from the governor's testimony is of interest. When asked if he saw any area of compromise between the Fisher Bill and the C T A bill, he replied, "No, I do not."

The governor was not alone in his enthusiasm for the Fisher Bill. A committee composed of academic professors called the Committee for Improving Teacher Education (C I T E) seems to have sprung up early in 1961. In February we find this committee urging citizens to support its resolutions, which were in general in favor of the Fisher Bill, but they asked that the bill be "strengthened." In this manifesto, the committee stated that "In Sacramento there are strong elements of support of the purposes of the Bill. However, in face of active counterpressures that support may waver. The voices of those who believe in the Bill must be heard." The intent of the bill, according to the C I T E was "to encourage and make it possible for able people to seek a career in public education."

According to the same group, the bill needed amendment to define "academic" so as to refer "only to majors in the natural sciences, the social sciences (other than education), the humanities, and such majors in the fine arts which, in the judgment of the State Board of Education, provide appropriate emphasis on the theory and history of the subject art." Another amendment, it was said, was needed "so that no more than 18 credits of professional preparation could be required for an elementary credential and no more than 15 for a general secondary credential, including directed teaching, *all* methods courses (in any department) and courses in audio-visual aids. To approve the foregoing limits is the maximum which training institutions could *require* of candidates for the credential."

One of the practices objected to by the supporters of the Fisher Bill seems to have been the appointment of teachers who had majored in physical education to positions as superintendents (the route being through the coaching staff). It seems to have been felt that, by requiring a real academic major for the secondary credential and then a secondary credential plus other requirements for the future superintendent, this practice could be stopped. A roundabout way of attempting a reform, it would appear.

As the hearings in the senate on the Fisher Bill proceeded, some of the difficulties always besetting reformers became apparent. Some hard questions had to be answered. How was it proposed to staff courses in industrial arts, home economics, agriculture, music, and physical education, not to mention the strictly vocational subjects? A blast from the California Industrial Education Association's Committee on Teaching Credentials brought a sense of reality into the discussion. At all events, the bill was repeatedly amended after various senate committee hearings, and as it went to the floor of the senate, it contained the following important provision, which was to lead to a bitter controversy *after* the bill became law: "A major and minor, one of which shall be in an academic subject matter area and one of which may be in a non-academic subject area, normally taught in the public schools." This certainly would seem to take care of the physical education and home economics teachers. But in so doing the bill seemed to fail to accomplish what some of its supporters wished. Could it be that these supporters had not thought through what they really wanted? An outsider cannot help feeling they had not done their homework.

The California Teachers Association and the California Council on Teacher Education were not in favor of the Fisher Bill. The latter, in a summary published in April 1961, pointed out that the bill violated the following principles:

> 1. Credential legislation should provide broad guidelines, leaving appropriate details to State Board credential regulation.
> 2. It is the responsibility of colleges and universities to determine programs for the preparation of teachers within the framework of legal requirements and accreditation.

These points involve an issue quite separate from the academic major and related topics—and to my mind this issue was the vital one. What was under dispute was the degree of delegation of authority by the legislature. What the teachers association failed to make clear is that a legislature will only delegate authority to a body in which the public has full confidence. Behind such an issue, however, lies another, namely the confidence of any given group in the body to which the authority is delegated.

With the governor behind the Fisher Bill, there was no difficulty in its passage through the senate (after many amendments to be sure). The assembly was another problem. According to the information I have received from several well-informed sources, the problem was to get the bill reported out favorably by the Assembly Committee on Education. To accomplish this, several Republican votes were essential, and at least one Republican member was particularly responsive to the views of the extreme right wing of his Party. An appeal calculated to elicit pressure from the extreme right on the committee members was sent out to the voters. The committee reported favorably and the bill was passed by the assembly in June 1961 and signed by the governor. A combination of Democratic votes loyal to the governor's program, the teachers union, and some right-wing Republican votes carried the day against the California Teachers Association, which had never been so defeated in memory of man.

The Fisher Bill was signed by the governor and became the law of the state. But the controversy over certification was by no means ended. The matter entered what I may call the area of bureaucratic struggle, which as I write is still in progress. An account of this battle would take me beyond the scope of this present chapter. Let me just remind the reader of the line-up of the contending forces during the legislative session of 1961. The initiative for the Fisher Bill came from people close to Governor Brown. The self-appointed Committee for the Improve-ment of Teacher Education (C I T E) started off lobbying with unrealistic demands; lined up with this lobby was the P T A, the members of the state board who had been appointed by Governor Brown, the Democratic leadership in the senate, and the state school boards association.

On the other side were those whom I have referred to as members of the establishment, the leaders of the state teachers associations, the administrators associations, and associations of teachers of the industrial arts, of agriculture, and physical education. It will be noted that as I have diagnosed the situation, the majority of the state board were in disagreement with the public school people. This would not have been the case a decade earlier. Indeed, in talking to many academic people in California in 1960, it became evident that they were unwilling to see power placed in the hands of a state board in spite of the changed composition of the board. For years the board, the chief state school officer, and the staff had been working hand in glove with the establishment. Few in California could believe that educational issues could be taken out of the legislature as in New York State and decided by a state authority which was friendly to the public school people but not dominated by them.

Higher Education East and West

I now turn from the discussion of shaping school policy in two states to a consideration of higher education. At once California stands out as the one state in the Union that has developed and put into operation a master plan. Whether one approves of the plan (as I do) or not is quite beside the point. What is encouraging about it, and makes that state worthy of study, is the fact that a long-range educational policy has been established. It is of more than passing interest that this success in the field of higher education was achieved at just the time when the defenders and critics of the public schools were wrestling in the legislature about the Fisher Bill. One cannot help trying to find an explanation for the apparent inconsistency in the two outcomes. Why was California able to set an example in shaping educational policy as regards colleges and universities at the very time when the question of who was to determine policy for the schools was at issue?

The answer, to my mind, is that in one case the contending forces came to an agreement between 1959 and 1961, *before* action by the legislature was considered. For if I were to go back into the history of higher education in California, I am sure I would find plenty of examples where vested educational interests were lobbying in the legislative halls. As compared with New York, California has suffered recently from a lack of confidence of the people of the state in those making policy for the schools. Hence the quarrel over certification that I have just described. No such lack of confidence existed as regards the state university. Quite the contrary, the university under the long and successful administration of President Sproul had been able to encompass the entire state. A threatened split into two or more separate universities some years ago had been prevented—no mean accomplishment, one must say. A single administration of many campuses had evolved and became accepted. The board of trustees (with the title of the Board of Regents) had the confidence of the legislators upon whom they depended for funds. The local two-year public colleges had come into existence some years before. Since World War II, the teachers colleges had become state colleges with a variety of programs. The private colleges and the two large and independent private universities were not competing for students (as most colleges had been in the depression years). The tremendous immigration into California was presenting all institutions, private and public, with too many applicants for admission.

The existence of one and only one state university was in a sense a master plan. But in the 1950s I heard the question raised more than once when I was visiting the state: What was to prevent one or more of the state colleges from becoming a state university? All that would be required for such action, so typical of the American scene, would be an act of the legislature. Another question one often heard was whether a community that supported a local two-year college would not exert sufficient pressure in the legislature to have the college "upgraded" to a four-year state college. Similar occurrences were happening all over the United States. In other words, more than one skeptical observer of the California picture in the 1950s predicted that the existing pattern would change drastically, particularly because of the vast increase in the school population then in progress. The question was: Could those who were interested in the local two-year colleges, the state colleges, the private institutions, and the university agree to a plan for the future? Though I have known something of the state over a period of forty years, I must say that my prophecy in, say, 1955 for agreement on a master plan would have been pessimistic.

Two stages of the development were essential. First there must be agreement among the leaders of the separate interests. Second the legislature must accept the agreement, not as a temporary compromise but as long-range policy, in short, a master plan. Note that here there would be no question of the legislature's delegating authority in this matter. The legislature had to appropriate funds for both the university and the state colleges, and the status and financing of the local two-year colleges was dependent on legislative action. However, the legislature did delegate its power of *exploring* the whole issue and laying plans for the future. In 1959 the legislature adopted a resolution asking the trustees of the university and the state Board of Education (responsible for the state colleges and, indirectly, for the two-year colleges) to prepare a master plan. This plan was to provide for "the development, expansion and integration of the facilities, curriculum, and standards of higher education, in junior colleges [two-year local colleges], state colleges, the University of California, and other institutions of higher education of the state, to meet the needs of the state during the next ten years and thereafter." A report was to be rendered within a year.

Following this resolution, a liaison committee of the state board and the trustees of the university appointed a Master Plan Survey Team of some eight persons representing private colleges, the state colleges, the public schools, the university, and the junior colleges. This survey team created technical committees that supplied much of the basic information. It was also able to start with a consideration of a report of a Joint Advisory Committee of eleven educators which had been created in joint resolution of the state board and the trustees of the university in 1959. This advisory committee had been charged with considering questions "concerning the coordination of public education in California . . . the establishment of additional campuses, and the relationship between the three segments of public higher education in respect to their functions, admission requirements, and programs in order to reduce unnecessary duplication of campuses, facilities and programs."

The report of this advisory committee, in which all the different educational interests were represented, was in itself a major accomplishment. For it set forth the "functions of the junior colleges, state colleges and the University of California" in quite precise terms, including the significant statement that the state college students would be drawn "from the upper 40 per cent and University students from the upper 15 per cent of all California public high school graduates." The survey team modified the statements of the Joint Advisory Committee in certain respects, and ended up with the following declaration of admission policies:

The junior colleges will:

Admit all graduates of California high schools who desire to continue their education and others whose maturity indicates potential success in post-high school education.

The state colleges will:

1. Admit students who typically rank in the upper 33⅓ per cent of all graduates of public high schools in California.
2. Admit qualified transfer students. [This means essentially from the junior colleges.]
3. Admit to graduate study qualified graduates of institutions of higher learning. [Ordinarily for the master's degree; see below.]

4. Expand upper division and graduate enrollments faster than the lower division enrollments.

The University of California will:

1. Admit students who typically rank in the upper 12½ per cent of all graduates of public high schools in California.
2. Admit qualified transfer students. [In practice this means a large number who have completed satisfactorily the academic program in the two-year junior colleges.]
3. Admit to graduate study qualified graduates of institutions of higher learning.
4. Expand upper division and graduate enrollments faster than the lower division enrollments.

In addition all three segments will:

Meet the special needs of superior students by co-operating with high schools in admitting certain gifted high school seniors to college courses while they are completing their high school work. Already sanctioned by law in the case of the junior colleges and followed by some campuses of the University, the practice should be authorized for the state colleges also.

In regard to *research*, the following procedure was finally adopted:

The junior colleges will:

Consider themselves instructional institutions with work confined to the lower divisions; hence, research should be directed toward improving the quality of junior college instruction. (In addition, junior college faculty should be encouraged to pursue individual research during summers and whenever possible during the academic year.)

The state colleges will:

1. Recognize that instruction is their paramount function and will provide library, laboratory, and other facilities appropriate to the degrees offered.

2. Carry on research, using facilities provided for and consistent with the primary function of the state colleges.

The University of California will:

1. Be the primary state-supported academic agency for research, both basic and applied.
2. Be the primary public repository for scarce documents and other unique library resources needed for the doctor's degree and for research programs.
3. As part of its responsibility for scholarly work, make its research and library facilities available to qualified members of faculties of other institutions.

A section of the report entitled "Instructional Functions" may be summarized as follows:

The junior colleges will provide two years of "a collegiate education for students planning to complete work for baccalaureate degrees [i.e., by transfer to a state college or the university] as well as two-year associate arts degree programs" with broad application for citizenship, health, family living, science, and basic communication needed by citizens, plus vocational-technical and general education and training "to prepare students for occupations which require two years of training or less."

The state college will provide "broad programs leading to the bachelor's degree" in a variety of fields and will "discharge their major responsibility for the preparation of teachers"; in addition they will provide programs of graduate study leading to the master's degree, and may award the doctoral degree jointly with the University of California. (The reader should note this important provision which, it is hoped, will regulate the expansion of the graduate work in the state colleges.)

The University of California will provide instruction leading to the bachelor's degree, master's degree, and doctoral degrees, and instruction in professional fields and programs for the preparation of teachers. The university

will "be the primary state-supported academic agency for
research." This provision together with the limitation on
the awarding of doctors' degrees by the state college are
important elements of the plan.

All the state colleges were to be considered as
constituting a state college system to be administered "by a
body corporate known as The Trustees of the State College
System of California." The board of trustees was to consist
of five ex-officio members and sixteen members appointed
by the governor for a term of sixteen years. It was further
recommended that there be created a "co-ordinating
Council for Higher Education" consisting of three representatives each from the university, the state college system,
the junior colleges, and the independent colleges and
universities. To this council were assigned the duties of
reviewing the current budget of the state college system and
the university, as well as performing a number of bursary
functions and developing plans "for the orderly growth of
public higher education."

A doubting Thomas can readily raise the question of
how well this coordinating Council for Higher Education
will function, and a closely related question, how long will
the master plan endure? In 1960 it was hoped by some of the
proponents that the basic principles of the master plan
would become part of the state constitution. If that action
had been taken the stability of the plan would have been
more readily assured. Actually the plan was put in operation
by a bill passed by overwhelming majorities in both houses
in a special session of the 1960 legislature. It contains most
of the features of the report of the survey team as accepted
by the liaison committee of the state board and the trustees
of the University of California, though one searches in vain
to find the details in regard to admission policies of the
survey team. Nevertheless, since these policies were
approved by representatives of all the interested parties,
they would seem to have the force of an unwritten law, and

one continually hears them referred to as part of the plan adopted by the legislature. Three important sections of the law do spell out the functions of the three types of public institutions as recommended by the survey team. They are as follows:

> [The university] is the primary state-supported academic agency for research. The University has the sole authority in public higher education to award the doctoral degree in all fields of learning, except that it may agree with the state colleges to award joint doctoral degrees in selected fields.
>
> The primary function of the state colleges is the provision of instruction for undergraduate students and graduate students, through the master's degree, in the liberal arts and sciences, in applied fields and in the professions, including the teaching profession.
>
> Public junior colleges shall offer instruction through but not beyond the fourteenth grade level, which instruction may include, but shall not be limited to, programs in one or more of the following categories: (1) standard collegiate courses for transfer to high institutions, (2) vocational and technical fields leading to employment, and (3) general or liberal arts courses. Studies in these fields may lead to the associate in arts or associate in science degrees.

To my mind California is to be loudly praised for having adopted a master plan for higher education and I would recommend that other states follow suit. I am not saying that the *details* of the California plan can or should be copied in all states. The flexibility of the scheme, however, is a feature that all states might well imitate. But in some other states, the state university (or universities) claims to be developing an equally flexible scheme by establishing two-year branches throughout the state. It is said that, for those planning to complete an undergraduate general program at the university itself, the instruction is superior in the two-year local branches to that provided by local independent two-year junior colleges. On the other hand, it seems doubtful if the vocational-technical two-year courses provided under the auspices of a university are likely to be as satisfactory as under the California arrangement. In states like Ohio, where there are many private liberal arts colleges, the movement for the creation of two-year colleges (or two-year extensions of a state university) is unlikely to receive much support. In many states there is also bound to be a certain fear on the part of state colleges with a four-year program of general content of competition by local junior colleges that would be tied into a university (as in California) through transfer into the junior year. In this connection it is interesting that the O E C D examiners expressed the opinion that "The private small college will occupy a less important place. The public junior college will emerge as the basis of a popular higher education." But in a footnote they add that "much will depend upon the energy and ingenuity with which liberal arts colleges pursue schemes for pooling resources to gain economies of scale, as for example in Claremont [California]".

In discussing the merits of the details of the California plan I have already wandered too far from the theme of this book, namely, How can the United States best shape educational policy? Let me point out again that the great merit of what was done in California lies in the fact that *a* master plan for higher education was worked out by competent committees and adopted by the legislature. The future of the United States would be brighter if all states began right now to follow this example. Yet only a few have done so. New York is one, and I conclude this chapter by noting the progress that has been made and recounting the difficulties as compared with California in bringing order into higher education.

First there is New York City, with its tradition of free city-supported higher education; second, the number of private colleges and universities is greater than in California, and their influence much greater; third, the development of local junior colleges has been slow and uncertain; fourth, until very recently the state colleges for training teachers have remained almost exclusively teachers colleges (as is the case in the neighboring states of Connecticut and New Jersey); finally and most important, a state university was only established after World War II, and there have been great difficulties—political, financial, and educational—in its development. In short, to produce a master plan for New York is quite a different undertaking from the task that faced Californians in 1959.

After considerable study and discussion, which was going on as far back as World War II, the 1961 legislature of the State of New York passed a law looking toward a state-wide plan. The Board of Regents was directed to follow certain specific procedures in planning for statewide coordination of higher education. Pursuant to the provisions of this law, in 1962 the board "activated" the Office of Planning for Higher Education in the state Department of Education. In January 1963 the office began actual operation.

As in the case of teacher certification, the legislature has turned to its ancient creation, the Board of Regents, for exploratory studies. The mode of operation at this stage of planning is quite different from that in California, just because a powerful state university was not already in existence. Indeed the whole development of state-supported higher education in New York is complicated by the high prestige and great success of the Board of Regents, which acts both as a board of education and as a watchdog over private and public institutions. On its creation in the eighteenth century, the board was thought of as the governing body of the University of the State of New York, and the title still remains. This university, however, has never functioned as state universities in other states, and the relation of the Board of Regents to the trustees of the more recent state university remains a problem.

At the time of this writing, New York is in the initial stages of statewide planning—some ten regional meetings have been held over the state and efforts have been made to develop channels of communication and mutual support among the three interested parties (the state university, the city university, and the private institutions). It is the hope of the Board of Regents and its administrative staff that a sufficient base of support can be mobilized and that as many issues as possible can be completely resolved prior to the submission of the master plan, scheduled for December 1964.

Although it is much too early to say what type of over-all plan New York will ultimately adopt in an effort to bring about a "rationalization" of its higher education efforts, the basic assumptions to guide long-range statewide planning in higher education have been substantially agreed upon. These premises include:

1. Opportunities in higher education in the fields of study chosen by a *sizable* number of full-time undergraduate students should be provided on a decentralized basis in every area of concentrated population. (The definition of concentrated population varies depending upon the field of study under consideration.) Opportunities in the fields of study chosen by a relatively *small* number of undergraduate students and by graduate students should be provided in one or more places on a centralized basis.

2. Decentralized opportunities provided in many places throughout the state should include courses covering at least the first two years of centralized opportunities. This will facilitate transfer of appropriate students into the junior year of centralized facilities.

3. At least the first two *preparatory* years of the following fields of study should be available in every area of concentrated population: liberal arts, teacher education, business and accounting, engineering, and collegiate nursing. (These five fields of study accounted for 82 per cent of certain high school seniors of 1953 who chose four-year colleges.)

4. The decentralized opportunities within an area may be provided by private colleges, public institutions, or both.

5. In any economic area in which private colleges appear to be unable to meet the need for decentralized facilities, the gap should be filled by publicly supported programs.

6. *Technical-Terminal* fields of study of two years duration or less should be provided also in every area of concentrated population where industrial and commercial demands require them. Consideration should be given to means by which such programs may be readily established in those localities where need exists. Such institutions would be of sufficient size and appropriate curriculum to meet the demands of industry and population.

7. In order to assure sufficient assistance for college attendance by superior youth of inadequate financial means and to retain a freedom of choice for the individual, an expanded Regents Scholarship program based on need as well as quality is essential.

8. Existing institutions represent a substantial investment in faculties, facilities, and experience. Since it is an obligation of the Board of Regents and the State University Trustees to recognize and foster the historical development of higher education in this State, which has been accomplished largely through the establishment and encouragement of private institutions, additional ways and means must be found to assist colleges and universities under private auspices to accommodate future enrollments. As a corollary, such assistance should serve to protect without dislocation or distraction the invaluable accumulated organic experience of the staffs of our existing institutions.

9. Needs in certain areas of the State appear to be so substantial that immediate action is required to provide the facilities needed.

Developments of a specific *modus operandi* to carry out the above objectives rests in the Office of Planning in Higher Education. To accomplish its basic goal of a sound long-range plan, the office is attempting to: (1) involve the responsible leadership of each institution as fully as possible; (2) fully utilize all extant data so that additional institutional research will be kept at a minimum; (3) establish "the process of planning on sound objective data and the best professional judgments that can be mustered."

Thus New York is starting down the California road. One can only applaud and wish for rapid progress. One might likewise hope that at the level of secondary education California might borrow from New York's example.

CHAPTER 5

Toward a Nationwide Educational Policy

As we have seen, educational policy in the United States has been determined in the past by the more or less haphazard interaction of (1) the leaders of public school teachers, administrators and professors of education, (2) state educational authorities, (3) a multitude of state colleges and universities, (4) private colleges and universities, and (5) the variety of agencies of the Federal government, through which vast sums of money (Table 3, Chart 1, page 13) have flowed to individual institutions and the states.

It is my thesis that such a jumble of influential private and public bodies does not correspond to the needs of the nation in the 1960s. Some degree of order needs to be brought out of this chaos, primarily for the benefit of the on-coming generations, but also, to achieve a more effective use of public and private moneys.

At the high school level and below, policy should not be determined solely by either "public school people" or state officials, but wise decisions cannot be made if either is excluded. At the level beyond the high school, plans cannot be made by the state alone, nor by private institutions alone, nor by Washington alone. But no nationwide policy can be successfully formulated if any one of the three is excluded. A single state, as the California action shows, can develop a master plan for higher education; any single state can, as New York has shown, keep its schools well up-to-date with the educational revolution. Congress can help meet the problems presented by the revolution by grants for specific purposes and a handsome assist to institutions of higher education. But all this does not add up to a nationwide educational policy, let alone a national educational policy which would be the equivalent of the national policy in Great Britain[1] or France.

The fact is, of course, that without a drastic Constitutional amendment nobody is in a position to establish an educational policy in the United States. It is my contention that some form of cooperative exploration of educational problems between the states and the Federal government is imperative. We cannot have a national educational policy, but we might be able to evolve a *nationwide policy*. The concluding pages of this chapter give my suggestions as to how this might be accomplished without an amendment to the Constitution of the United States. Before presenting my radical proposal, however, I must devote some pages to an analysis of the present situation.

Let me start with an examination of the powers of the Federal government to establish a national educational policy through the formation of a commission or committee appointed by the Congress or the President. Until one

---

[1] The report of the committee appointed by the prime minister under the chairmanship of Lord Robbins "to review the pattern of full-time higher education" is an excellent example of long range flexible planning. The report was published late in 1963 and has received wide support.

examines the Constitutional and political realities, such proposals seem quite persuasive. And it is true, of course, that for more than 100 years Congress, by its granting of land or its appropriation of money for the individual states, has enormously influenced the development of our educational system. But Congress has not the power, without an amendment to the Federal Constitution, to determine a total national educational policy. Why not? Because in government, as in business, authority to establish a policy requires full power (1) to establish a structure and to alter it as conditions change; (2) to appoint personnel; (3) to issue directions to the personnel; (4) to provide for the financing of the entire operation. It is the essence of our system of government, with its checks and balances and division of powers, that neither a single state nor the Federal government has the power to establish, maintain, and operate a system of education in the way a free nation without a federalized structure can establish educational policy.

The educational powers of each of the single states in practice is far greater than that of the Federal government. There are, however, three limitations on these powers. The first derives from the Federal Constitution as interpreted by the Supreme Court; the second is the power of Congress to pass laws affecting individuals as citizens of the United States, as for example the power to draft men into military service; the third is the practical limitations of a state's ability to raise money. There are a number of recent examples of Supreme Court decisions that limit the power of a state to determine its educational policy. These decisions, which have attracted widespread interest, involve the Court's interpretation of the First and Fourteenth Amendments of the Federal Constitution. The questions they raise concern state and local provisions as to the use of school time for ceremonies or instruction considered to be religious. It is interesting to note that no one now argues that a state would be free to establish a state-supported system of schools which were frankly connected with a religious denomination. Yet before the Fourteenth Amendment was passed after the Civil War, such a possibility existed, since the First Amendment originally was only a limitation on the power of the Federal government.

The decisions of the Supreme Court on racial segregation in the schools are clearly a limitation on a state's power to establish and maintain completely separate Negro schools, colleges, and universities. One of the earliest decisions in which the Court reversed a state educational policy held that the Fourteenth Amendment guaranteed to a parent a right to send his children to a private school of his own choice, notwithstanding any state law. The attempt of a state legislature (Oregon) to outlaw private schools was thus thwarted. The same issue had arisen in a less dramatic form in Nebraska, where the state legislature had by law regulated the teaching of foreign languages. The Court held that the legislature could not prevent a private school from offering instruction in German, since to do so would be to deprive a parent of a right to have his child so instructed. The power of the state to regulate the curriculum of the public schools was not contested.

The impact of Federal legislation for purposes of defense on schools and colleges was clearly evident during the two World Wars. The drafting of young men into the armed services does, in a sense, place a restriction on the power of the state to plan the education of its young people. To a certain extent the same may be said of Federal laws affecting the employment of youth in industries engaged in interstate commerce.

The greatest limitation on the ability of the state to provide for education of its youth at public expense comes from the limitations on the ability of the state to raise funds. (One need not dwell on the restraints imposed by the Federal Constitution, such as the prohibition of post-facto laws and the requiring of due process; these stand as a guard against arbitrary confiscation of personal property.) The practical limitations of the Federal income tax are most often in the minds of educators when they discuss the impact of the Federal power on state power. A generation ago conservative school people, deeply committed to the principle of local control of the public schools, openly deplored the amendment which authorized the Federal income tax. This amendment, it was said, would destroy the basic structure of our public schools.

There can be no doubt that the Federal taxing power, broadened by the Sixteenth Amendment, does mean that a state is not as independent a sovereign power as it once was insofar as supporting state activities is concerned. Not only does the Federal government absorb a large portion of the income available for taxation, but the methods by which some of this money is sent back to the states affects indirectly the way the state spends what money it collects. I refer to such measures as the Federal road-building program. The basis for this program is such that state funds are drawn into this type of expenditure because Federal money comes to the state only if the state itself provides money for the same purpose. The advocates of general Federal aid for public education have made much of the implication of such arrangements, and this argument has never been adequately answered by the opponents of Federal aid.

In writing of the limitations of the power of a state to establish an educational policy, I have made no reference to the state constitutional limitations on the power of the state legislature and the organs of government created by the legislature, such as the local school boards. In theory, the people of a state can change their constitution; therefore, in contrasting state with Federal power, it is unnecessary to consider the state constitution. This is fortunate as I doubt if the provisions of any two of the fifty state constitutions are alike, even on such basic matters as schools and colleges.

Because of the Federal Constitution and certain rights of the Federal government connected with defense and interstate commerce, it is evident that a state is not completely free to provide and regulate education. On the other hand, let it be noted that the Federal government is powerless to interfere with many aspects of state-supported schools, colleges, and universities. It has been pointed out more than once that a state need not provide any public instruction at all. Some states have no compulsory attendance laws. Therefore one might say that it is a happy accident that in all states, at present, there are free public schools and at least one state university and several state colleges. It is further a happy accident that in all but a few states children must attend school (public or private) from approximately six years of age until at least sixteen (in some states until eighteen).

An example of the impotence of the Federal government in school affairs is illustrated by the attempts of the executive branch in 1963 to remedy the situation which had existed since 1959 in Prince Edward County, Virginia. The public schools in this county were closed because those in control of raising local funds preferred that the schools be closed rather than be integrated following the order of a Federal court. A long litigation ensued involving both state and Federal courts. The government in Washington made it clear that it considered the situation intolerable. For four years there had been no free schools in Prince Edward County; white children were being educated in private schools, Negro children were receiving no education. Offhand, one would think the Administration would have opened free schools in that county. But I have been informed that experts in Constitutional law believe that the Federal government has no power to open and operate a school within a state. (Federal power in the District of Columbia is another matter.) Therefore a private corporation with private funds was established.

In the depression days there were those in Washington who seemed ready to establish a system of Federally controlled schools. As a consequence, the leaders of public education issued a vigorous warning of the danger of the Federal government's taking over our system of public schools and thus replacing local control and diversity with a monolithic uniformity.

A commission of prominent educational leaders wrote in March 1945 as follows:

> The National Youth Administration was the farthest advance of the Federal Government into the field of educational control during the depression. . . . In the N Y A the national government set up its own organization responsible for the direct administration of youth education. The Federal officers in charge soon made it clear, however, that it was to be a permanent agency. The N Y A began to establish schools of its own in direct competition with established public school systems.

The commission then reminded the reader that even after the entry of the United States into World War II, the N Y A was abolished "by Congress only after a hard fight and by a close vote." A few paragraphs later, the authors wrote:

> It is the mature conclusion of the Commission responsible for the issuance of this report that a continuance of recent and current trends in Federal-state relations in education will, within a measurable period of time, transfer predominant responsibility for the control of education in the United States from the states and localities to the national government. Already we have traveled further along this road than generally realized.[1]

[1] "Federal-State Relations in Education," March, 1945. A joint report of the Educational Policies Commission (appointed by the National Education Association and the American Association of School Administrators) and the Committee on Problems and Policies of the American Council on Education.

Few today remember these fears. Except for military academies and schools for Indians and educational establishments in the District of Columbia, the Federal government has not established Federal institutions. Quite apart from the Constitutional question, as a practical political matter I cannot imagine Congress voting to charter and support a degree-granting institution in any state. For such an institution would clearly be in competition with state-supported institutions.

We can dismiss any talk of the Federal government establishing and operating a Federal system of schools or even a single school or college or university in one of the fifty sovereign states. Clearly a government without the power to establish educational institutions is hardly in a position to establish a national educational policy. I might note in passing that even if Congress should charter and support a college or establish a school, such an institution's activities would be subject to the Constitutional provisions as interpreted by the Supreme Court. Such a college, for example, could not be connected with a religious denomination, nor could it exclude students because of race or religion.

One thus comes out with the simple but disconcerting fact that there can be no national educational policy and only within limits can we speak of fifty state educational policies. This fact, I believe, has been too little faced in most discussions of what to do about our schools, colleges, and universities. It has been often assumed in recent years that the Congress could establish a national educational policy because it had the first call on the taxable wealth of the nation. There can be no question, as I have already said, that the acts of Congress have greatly influenced educational policy in all the states. One might call this a Federal policy made possible by continuous bribery. Such a policy has its limitations, but first let us explore some of the ways in which educational reformers have achieved their ends by persuading Congress to grant money to the states for specific educational purposes.

During the period just before the Civil War, there was widespread interest in the United States in new educational developments focused on education for practical purposes. The private colleges such as Harvard, Yale, Princeton, William and Mary, and also the state universities such as Virginia and the University of Michigan, were heavily criticized because they were still deeply committed to the classical or literary tradition. The legislatures of two states —Michigan and Pennsylvania—in the 1850s established new colleges for the education of agriculturists and engineers. Under the impact of the reform movement, Yale and Harvard established scientific schools alongside the traditional colleges. However, the pace of change was too slow to suit the forward-looking people of that time. The power of the purse of the Federal government was appealed to with the result that in the midst of the Civil War the Morrill Act was passed. The Federal government was rich in land, and from these riches each state received a portion for the purpose of promoting education in agriculture and the mechanical arts.

The first measure to establish what came to be known as the land-grant colleges was vetoed by President Buchanan because he believed that even influencing the states indirectly by grants of Federal money (in the form of land) was un-Constitutional. Nobody would have entertained the idea that Congress could *direct* the state governments to add to their state universities a school of agriculture and a school of engineering. Yet in terms of formulating an educational policy this is what a majority of the Congress desired (either that or the establishment of a separate state college for the same purposes). The Morrill Act was passed before the Fourteenth Amendment was even thought of. But wide as the powers of the Federal government have become due to this amendment, no one suggests today any more than in the 1850s that Congress can direct the states as to how each state shapes its educational policy. The reformers who wish to invoke the power of the Federal government must do so by invoking the power of the purse. This power is exercised, let it be noted, not by withholding funds but by tempting the state to new endeavors by offering Federal funds to cover *part* of the expenses.

The second important successful attempt to change the course of educational history by an Act of Congress was the Smith-Hughes Act of 1907. This act was passed because of the pressure of earnest people connected with labor, management, and public education. Federal funds were allocated to the states to be used for providing vocational education, provided each state also put in some of its own funds. As matters developed over the years in this case, as in the case of the land-grant colleges, the state ended by paying a large portion of the total bill. One might classify these two acts of Congress (and subsequent Acts connected with the same effort) as pump-priming operations, though it is interesting to note that in 1957 $83.9 million of Federal funds went to the land-grant institution (Table 3, page 13).

In this century, philanthropic organizations have followed the same course. An initial grant of money to an institution, it is hoped and believed, will result in the establishment of a new educational endeavor which before long will be supported entirely by the institution itself. Such efforts (on the whole successful) would fall under the heading "educational reform through philanthropic bribery."

The third important use of the power of the Federal purse to influence educational policy was the National Defense Education Act of 1958. The passage of the act again underscores the impotence of the Federal government to regulate education or even guide its development. The act as finally passed was a composite law with provisions to suit a variety of pressure groups. The one provision most likely to improve secondary education was cast aside, because neither the leaders of the public school people nor the politicians would support it. I have in mind the allocation to each state of Federal money to improve the instruction in five subjects in grades 7 through 12, namely English, mathematics, science, foreign languages, and social studies (including history). The improvement contemplated was smaller classes and higher salaries for the teachers of these academic subjects. The idea of a differentiation of salaries among teachers based on subject taught or the grade level has always been anathema to the N E A.

Let us stop a moment to consider what other measures Congress could conceivably have passed at the time when public opinion was clamoring for an improvement of the secondary education of the academically talented. At first sight it would seem conceivable that Congress might have passed a law establishing examining bodies not unlike those which in England administer the examinations for the "General Education Certificate," and provided somehow that all or almost all the bright students would take these examinations. The catch in this conception is the word "somehow." What sanctions could Congress enact that would be effective? A state legislature in theory could require that all students in grade 12 of the state-supported schools (the public schools) take a set of examinations, or at least as in New York State now, take a certain set of examinations if they wish to obtain a special type of diploma. A state legislature or its agent, a state board of education, can determine the curriculum of a public school. Failure to conform to the requirements can mean the closing of the school or at least the withdrawal of state funds, leaving the school to get on only with local tax support.

The powers of the state are clear at least in theory. Contrast the situation of the Federal government. One wonders what the chance would be of persuading Congress to pass a law tying appropriations to the admission of students on the basis of passing of examinations prescribed by a Federal commission. One may even question whether making the appropriation of Federal funds for educational purposes (say under the Smith-Hughes Act) dependent on the use of Federal examinations would be Constitutional. Without appearing to belabor an obvious point I do wish to emphasize how reformers intent on using the Federal power have repeatedly been forced to use what I have called "Federal bribery" to accomplish their purposes. To some extent, the legislatures in some states have used the same device to persuade local boards of education to change their educational policy. But these are exceptions. The state has the power (subject to the limitations I have noted) to establish educational policy as it sees fit.

We are not alone in facing difficult educational problems resulting from the federal nature of our government. The constitution of the Federal Republic of Germany places responsibility for education on each of the eleven states. It is interesting for Americans, therefore, to note how that country has handled the situation. Three organizations have been developed which to some degree serve to reduce the problems created by the federal structure. I refer to the Conference of Ministers of Education of the eleven states, which has a permanent secretariat; the Conference of the Heads of the Universities; and the Scientific Council, established in 1957 by a formal agreement between the separate states with each other and the federal government. The Scientific Council has published a series of recommendations and suggestions about the expansion of the universities and the founding of new universities. While the reports of this body have not been radical enough to suit some critics, they have served as a basis for action by the separate states. It is important to note that the state legislatures have been ready to respond to the recommendations largely because the Scientific Council was a creation of the governments of the separate states and the federal government.

In general I am convinced that educational systems cannot be exported or imported either as a whole or in part. Nevertheless I cannot help raising the question whether we do not need in the United States to create some sort of organization which will have the confidence of the state governments on the one hand, and on the other can bring to a focus a discussion of the important topics in education. Indeed I would hope there would be eventually not only a discussion but interstate cooperation.

An initial step along such a road was taken in 1949 with the establishment by sixteen states of the Southern Regional Education Board. Later (in 1953) came the formation of the Western Interstate Commission for Higher Education (thirteen states) and still later the New England Board of Higher Education (six states). Two of these regional boards or commissions are based on formal interstate compacts approved by Congress. Originally it was planned to have the Southern Regional Board also based on an interstate compact approved by Congress, but the idea was abandoned and its status is now that of an interstate agreement. All three agencies now embrace thirty-five states, leaving only twelve Midwestern states, in addition to New York, New Jersey, and Pennsylvania, outside any regional compact. A resolution urging the exploration of proposals for an interstate compact was adopted in 1954 by the Midwestern Regional Conference of the Council of State Governments. But in 1955 the committee reported against the proposal. Three years later eleven of the leading universities in the same area (including two private universities) formed the private voluntary organization known as the Committee on Institutional Cooperation. The chief purpose of this committee is to "improve the educational and public services offered by its member institutions while minimizing the cost of these services by fostering cooperation in instruction and research, particularly at the graduate level."

Clearly, both organizations created by agreement only and by interstate compact have a wider aim than can be possible for the association of a small group of universities. Indeed, one of the prime motives for the formation of these regional interstate planning commissions was the idea of improving and increasing educational opportunities for all the youth in the states involved. This it is hoped will be accomplished by the establishment of coordinated educational programs. As one person has well said, "We believed that we could better meet some of the problems in higher education by cooperation between the states rather than by competition."

The boards created by these interstate compacts are in theory at least regional planning agencies for higher education. None, I believe, has any authority or control over state activities or other educational institutions. However, by gathering facts and figures and identifying problems, the members of the staff can acquaint educators, legislators, and the public with the problems the region faces; expert consultants can recommend solutions. What has been achieved has been through persuasion, since no authority by coercion is even implied in the arrangement.

An example provided by the New England Board is typical of the good that may be accomplished in this manner. Facts made available to a university president in one state made it possible for him to withstand local pressures to establish a new program in a specialized area. He could point out that a similar program in the university in another state was already well developed and available. The objective is to prevent (by persuasion) a proliferation of programs and curricula when the needs of the region do not require them. The New England Board endeavors to bring into conferences legislative leaders as well as governors, budget officers, and educators to discuss programs throughout the area.

The work of these interstate boards is clearly only in its first stages, but the results, at least in some cases, show much promise. At the post-high-school level, where state differences are so great, at least some coordination of the diverse interests in a region may be possible. It is interesting to note that in all these interstate activities the emphasis is on education beyond the high school—indeed in most instances exclusively in this area. The reasons are evident. The forces I have already referred to have produced a considerable degree of uniformity in the schools. Out of this uniformity within each state has come a belief that the financing of the schools, in contrast to the state colleges and universities, was largely a matter of teachers' salaries. And the teachers' organizations have operated to reinforce this idea. The consequence has been that at least until recently there has appeared to be no reason for any official arrangement for the exchange of information about school problems and school finances among the states.

The states that have entered into these interstate compacts have certainly taken important steps in the direction of a rational approach to our educational problems. But one is still bound to ask: Are these regional pacts enough? They are excellent in principle and could be most effective in operation, but why only regional agreements? Why not a new venture in cooperative federalism? Why not a compact among *all* the states?

To be quite specific, let me be bold and make a suggestion for a possible way by which the road to the development of a nationwide educational policy might be opened up. *Let the fifty states, or at least fifteen to twenty of the more populous states, enter into a compact for the creation of an "Interstate Commission for Planning a Nationwide Educational Policy."* The compact would have to be drawn up by the states and approved by Congress. The document would provide for the membership of the commission and provide the guidelines for its operation. Each state would be represented, though a group of less populous states might decide to be represented by one person. Each state would be ready to listen to any conclusions of the commission but, of course, would not be bound to follow its recommendations.

Since such an interstate commission would be concerned with the drawing up of plans, *not* with administration, I see no constitutional or legal reason against a state legislature authorizing one or more persons to participate in it. Nor do I see any obstacles to a legislature expressing its willingness to examine any reports coming from such a group. The matter of finances might raise issues. It might be difficult to get any considerable number of state legislatures to appropriate the money; but I hope not, for if it were proposed that the Congress of the United States do so, certainly the cry of states' rights might be raised. Yet I would hope the commission would invite the chief United States school officer, the Commissioner of Education, as well as other Federal officials to attend each conference.

The whole commission, of course, would meet only from time to time. The real work would be done by special committees appointed by the commission, which might be called working parties. I suggest as a motto for all the working parties: "More facts, fewer slogans." And to get the facts and set them forth clearly on a state-by-state basis is a task, I submit, that has not yet been performed. For example, an interesting study published by the National Science Foundation (*The Duration of Formal Education for High Ability Youth*, N S F 61—36) indicates that on a national basis an alarmingly small percentage of able boys and girls go on to education in college and finish college. The study was preliminary and the statistics were obtained on a sampling basis. What is badly needed is more adequate data state by state. Such information would be basic to the work of *all* the working parties. In some states the most pressing need in terms of recruiting the academically talented students for the professions is to insure that more of this group finish high school and at least enter college. Throughout the preceding pages I have mentioned our lack of statistical information about the education of professional people state by state and their subsequent employment. We also lack in any one document a collection of the facts about scholarships and loans and the location of centers for study beyond the A. B. degree in relation to the distribution of the population. The increasing costs of education (Table 5, page 79) underline the importance of providing undergraduate and graduate education within commuting distance of home for as many young people as possible. There seems no doubt that the proximity of institutions of higher education is a factor in determining the level of college and university attendance. Some of the information needed, particularly about the impact of Federal spending, would be made available to the commission as a whole at first and used by the separate working parties as might be needed.

I am well aware there is no novelty in suggesting the appointment of a national body to plan for the future of American education. It is a time-honored scheme to have the President of the United States appoint a commission of educators and well-known laymen. This was done by President Hoover in 1930. His committee was charged as follows: "In view of the considerable differences of opinion as to policies which should be pursued by the Federal government with respect to education, I have appointed a committee representative of the important educational associations and others to investigate and present recommendations" (Annual Message to Congress, December 3, 1929).

The committee was chaired by the Secretary of the Interior, Ray Lyman Wilbur, who was president of

Stanford University on leave of absence. Three volumes of findings were published of which the last was entitled *Education in the States* and contained a wealth of statistical information. The recommendations, however, following the Presidential directive, were confined to action by the Federal government. It is ironical that the key recommendation, which found wide support among public school people then and now, has been blindly ignored by the national executive and Congress alike. The recommendation, in essence, was that no additional laws be passed "to grant federal financial aid to the States in support of special types of education."

The committee recognized that much good had been accomplished in the past by the special appropriations such as those for vocational education and to the land-grant colleges. Nevertheless they recommended that after a period of years all future grants of Federal money should be in "aid of education in general expendable by each state for any or all educational purposes as the state itself may direct." This was a statesmanlike but totally unrealistic recommendation, as the history of the next thirty years was to demonstrate. If accepted it would have blocked all efforts of reformers to use the power of Congress to appropriate money to promote the projects dear to their own hearts. Indeed, without the creation of some new coordinating political machinery, it would have so decentralized planning for education as to have made impossible many advances we now all praise. Nevertheless, as far as elementary and secondary education is concerned, I think the nation would have been better off if the views of the committee had prevailed. What became known as "general Federal aid for the public schools" was in line with the thinking of the members of Hoover's committee. The idea has been pushed for over thirty years by the N E A. There have been difficulties in deciding on what basis such general aid should be distributed to the states, but the chief opposition has come from the supporters of the church-connected elementary and secondary schools who wished to have their schools included. I have always been one of those strongly opposed to the use of taxpayers' money for private elementary and secondary schools (whether church-connected or not), because I believe it would lead to a fragmentation of our public schools as instruments for strengthening our democracy. The same argument does not apply to education beyond the high school, for our private colleges already enroll a large percentage of our youth. Furthermore, unlike the comprehensive high school, they have rarely set out to promote an understanding between cultural and economic groups within a local community.

Another Presidential committee was appointed by President Truman and still another by President Eisenhower. Both committees worked industriously and produced interesting, forward-looking documents, but one must use a microscope to find any evidence today of the effects of their recommendations. There exists in the statute books today authorization for the appointment of a national committee and there was recently introduced into Congress a bipartisan bill to authorize a "National Advisory Council on Education." Congressman Lindsay in speaking of the bill said, "We need to know what kind of educational programs are most vital to the welfare of America and most essential at this time." To which I venture to agree wholeheartedly and add we must know the programs in detail and how they can conceivably be implemented state by state. For example, the Congressman goes on to say that what the American people want to know are what kinds of priorities should be established among the many proposals requiring public funds—for example, youth employment, vocational education training, quality education, technical education, etc. Again I agree, but to me such priorities cannot be realistically determined except on a state-by-state basis. What Vermont has and what Vermont needs is very different in many areas from what California needs, which is different again from New Jersey. Therefore I suggest that Congress appoint first a National Advisory Committee to explore the workings of the present interstate compacts and to list the problems to be met. I am frank to say that I believe the report of such a preliminary survey would lead to the formation of the type of commission I have recommended based on an interstate compact.

I must admit that the record of national committees on education, however authorized and however appointed, is not such as to lead one to be optimistic about the results to be accomplished by still another committee. Yet the creation of a national commission which would be an interstate educational planning commission whose existence was the result of a compact between the states would be something quite new. It differs from schemes for appointing a Presidential or Congressional advisory commission in several respects. In the first place, because the commission would be an interstate commission, the reports of the working parties would be automatically concerned with state-by-state variations and would recognize the realities of the conditions in each state. In the second place, the recommendations would be directed to the state legislatures or state boards of education and would be considered by the state authorities because each state had been involved in the creation of the undertaking. In the third place, the magnitude and detailed nature of the financial demands required would be spelled out in such a way that Congress (through its own committees) and the Office of Education (through its own staff) could explore the significance of each item in terms of the function of the Federal governmental agencies.

Each working party would have to start with certain premises agreed upon by the commission. Within the framework thus established, the working party would be required first to make an exhaustive factual study of the structure state by state, second to come up with specific recommendations to the state authorities (the chief state school officer, the state school board, or the legislature). There might well be dissenting opinions on many points. The right to public dissent would be inherent in accepting an appointment on the working party. The more controversial the area, the more necessary would be such a provision.

Admittedly, in setting up any working party, the most difficult task for the interstate commission would be an agreement on what I have called the framework. And to let a working party loose in any controversial area without some guidelines would be to insure catastrophic failure at the onset. Certain premises could be agreed on without much difficulty. These would constitute part of the framework for all of the working parties. In my opinion, these premises might be formulated somewhat as follows:

1. It is assumed that our present form of government should be perpetuated; to that end all future citizens of the nation should receive an education that will prepare them to function as responsible members of a free society, as intelligent voters and, if appointed or elected to public office, as honest reliable servants of the nation, state, or locality.

2. It is assumed that each state is committed to the proposition of providing free schooling to all the children in the state through twelve grades. (Though the Federal government has no power to proclaim the doctrine of free schools, practically the action of all the states during the last 100 years enables the interstate commission to declare that providing free public schooling is a nationwide policy of the United States.)

3. It is assumed that in every state the parents have a right to send their children to private schools, colleges, and universities instead of to the publicly supported institutions.

This assumption follows from the interpretation of the Federal Constitution by the Supreme Court on more than one occasion.

4. It is assumed that each state *desires* to have all normal children in the state attend school at least five hours a day, 150 days a year, at least until they reach the age of 18, but that the states differ and will continue to differ in regard to the laws requiring school attendance and the way special provisions are provided for physically and mentally handicapped children.

5. It is assumed that each state accepts the responsibility of providing for the education of at least some of its youth beyond high school; the organization and financing of such education, however, differs and will continue to differ state by state; in each state opportunities for education beyond high school now include at least one university chartered by the state and largely supported by public funds; the continuation of such universities as centers of research, advanced study, and above all, fearless free inquiry is essential to the welfare of the state and the nation.

6. It is assumed that the education provided in high school and beyond by public institutions is designed to develop the potentialities of all the youth to fit them for employment in a highly industrialized society.

7. The financing of education, including research and scholarly work in the universities, is a concern of private universities, the states, and the Federal government.

The declaration of some such set of premises by an interstate commission would be the first step in shaping a nationwide educational policy. If each state legislature would pass a resolution accepting such a declaration, we should for the first time as a nation be officially committed to certain basic principles of educational policy. We now assume these principles to be valid, but in fact they have never been promulgated by representative assemblies and could not be promulgated by the Congress.

After formulating the premises of American education (the framework, as I have called it), the commission would determine what subjects to explore and name the working parties. Then many months later the commission would reconvene to receive the reports of the working parties, discuss them, and pass them on with comment to the legislatures of all the states represented. The working committees should be what the name implies. Their composition should be such as to represent diverse views of experts, and unanimous reports would *not* be expected. The layman's criticism would best come, I should think, from the interstate planning commission, which I envisage as being made up of distinguished citizens of each state who are *not* educators (the sort of person one finds on boards of trustees of our most famous universities). An alternate scheme in which the working parties contained laymen as well as educators need not be excluded.

However the working parties are composed, they should proceed to explore in depth the differences state by state and put these differences at the center of the debate when it came to making recommendations. If this were done, it would be almost certain that there would be different recommendations for different states, though one would hope not fifty in each case! How many working parties should be set up is a question. The topics which might be considered could be as many as twenty-five or thirty. But the scheme should not be endangered by an excessive burden of work. Merely as illustration, therefore, I suggest at the outset, working parties devoted to the following seven areas, without implying priorities:

1. Education in grades 13 and 14 (junior colleges) and the relation of this education to (a) professional training in a university and (b) the need for technicians. I have heard more than once that, as a nation, we are in short supply of the kind of person who is trained in some European countries in a course that is more practical and less scientific

than the usual four-year engineering course in the United States. This working party would, of course, consider the supply and demand of technical personnel, and would have to be in close contact with the second and third parties on the list.

2. Education for employment immediately on leaving high school, including vocational courses in high school and post-high school.

3. Science and engineering, including an inquiry into supply and demand of those prepared for research and development and the facilities available for training such personnel.

4. The education of the Negro.

5. The education of members of the medical profession.

6. Uniformity of standards for degrees beyond the master's degree.

7. The promotion of research and scholarly endeavors in *all* fields in our institutions of higher education.

I hardly need point out that problems of finance would be encountered by all the working parties. One would also meet the problem of Federal aid to private colleges and universities already alluded to in Chapter 3, and the present concentration of Federal funds for research in a relatively few centers. There are those who might consider the financial implications of the conclusions of the working parties and of the commission as a whole the most significant part of the undertaking. To quote once again from the O E C D report:

The task of financing the expansion of higher education is formidable. It is unlikely to be solved by recourse to private sources; the poorer states will look increasingly for general fiscal aid to the federal government and pressure is likely to mount for general aid to higher education. . . . If, as we think, the question of research support should in principle be separated from the question of aid to teaching in higher education, then those programs which are designed to spread the net for talent and to help the poorer states would be seen more clearly as contributing towards the building of a strong popular and national system of national education.

To which one can agree but point out that since the creation and location of new centers for higher education is a state affair, any approach to the questions raised by the O E C D examiners must be *in part* on a state-by-state basis.

There is a vast complex of interconnected questions to be answered before one can make a start at developing a rational *nationwide* educational policy. In raising and answering the questions, university faculties, administrators, state and Federal officials must be concerned. In the last analysis in many instances vital decisions must be made by the duly elected legislative bodies. Therefore in the early stages of the inquiry representatives of the lay public must play an active part, for what is needed is something far removed from institutional bargaining. What is needed is a national inquiry initiated by the elected representatives of the people in fifty states.

The O E C D examiners may or may not be right when they conclude "that the federal government ought to become a major source [of funds] by *direct contribution to the teaching functions of higher education.*" But I for one agree with the reply of one member of the American delegation who answered an examiner's question about the extent to which the Federal government can stimulate or initiate statewide planning. The Under-Secretary of the U. S. Department of Health, Education and Welfare, Mr. Nestingern said "that the momentum for developments of this kind must be generated at the state level with the cooperation of local communities. Under the American system this cannot be done by the Federal government, which is not in a position to initiate state planning." And he added that the Office of Education could encourage planning and help in the development of state plans.

To generate momentum at the state level requires that each state put its educational planning machinery in good order. To this end, I conclude this book by appealing to all citizens concerned with education to make their voices heard at the state capitals. To the end that more order be introduced into the present national picture, I appeal to members of state legislatures and of the Congress to examine the need for some sort of interstate cooperation. Anyone who examines the facts I have presented in the preceding pages will be convinced, I feel sure, of the need of more detailed state-by-state study of American education. For only by such a study, looking forward to prompt action, can we arrive at a *nationwide policy* adequate to meet the challenges of the new and awesome age in which we live.

Index

ABOUT THE AUTHOR

Dr. James Bryant Conant is an internationally known and respected scholar, scientist, statesman, and author. A former President of Harvard University, he has written more than a dozen books, including the famous *Slums and Suburbs*, which appeared in 1961, *The American High School Today*, published in 1959, and most recently, *The Education of American Teachers*. All three volumes were published by McGraw-Hill, and are ranked high among the significant works on education that have been written in recent years. When Dr. Conant returned to the United States from his post as Ambassador to Germany, he devoted himself to extensive studies of the American educational scene, working under a grant from the Carnegie Corporation. He has now returned to Free Berlin with the support of the Ford Foundation to advise the city government on educational matters.

DATE DUE
